WOMEN AND RELIGION IN THE FIRST CHRISTIAN CENTURIES

Women and Religion in the First Christian Centuries focuses on religion during the period of Roman imperial rule and its significance in women's lives. It discusses the rich variety of religious expression, from pagan cults and classical mythology to ancient Judaism and early Christianity, and the wide array of religious functions fulfilled by women. The author analyses key examples from each context, creating a vivid image of this crucial period which laid the foundations of western civilization.

The study challenges the concepts of religion and of women in the light of postmodern critique. As such, it is an important contribution to contemporary gender theory. In its broad and interdisciplinary approach, this book will be of interest to students of early religion as well as all those involved in cultural theory.

Deborah F. Sawyer is Senior Lecturer in the Department of Religious Studies at Lancaster University, where she directs a Masters programme in Women and Religion. Her publications include *Midrash Aleph Beth* (1993) and *A Walk in the Garden: Biblical, Iconographical and Literary Images of Eden* (1992).

RELIGION IN THE FIRST CHRISTIAN CENTURIES

Edited by Deborah Sawyer,

University of Lancaster,

and John Sawyer,

University College of St Martin, Lancaster

Too often the religious traditions of antiquity are studied in isolation, without any real consideration of how they interacted. What made someone with a free choice become an adherent of one faith rather than another? Why might a former pagan choose to become a 'God-fearer' and attend synagogue services? Why might a Jew become a Christian? How did the mysteries of Mithras differ from the worship of the Unconquered Sun, or the status of the Virgin Mary from that of Isis, and how many gods could an ancient worshipper have? These questions are hard to answer without a synoptic view of what the different religions offered.

The aim of the books in this series is to survey particular themes in the history of religion across the different religions of antiquity and to set up comparisons and contrasts, resonances and discontinuities, and thus reach a profounder understanding of the religious experience in the ancient world. The first topics to be covered will include: women; sacred languages and sacred texts; ritual and sacrifice; purity.

WOMEN AND RELIGION IN THE FIRST CHRISTIAN CENTURIES

Deborah F. Sawyer

London and New York

First published 1996
by Routledge
11 New Fetter Lane, London EC4P 4EE

Simultaneously published in the USA and Canada
by Routledge
29 West 35th Street, New York, NY 10001

Routledge is an International Thomson Publishing company
© 1996 Deborah F. Sawyer

Typeset in Garamond by
Ponting–Green Publishing Services, Chesham, Bucks
Printed and bound in Great Britain by
TJ Press (Padstow) Ltd, Padstow, Cornwall

British Library Cataloguing in Publication Data
A catalogue record for this book is available from
the British Library

Library of Congress Cataloguing in Publication Data
Sawyer, Deborah F., 1956–
Women and religion in the first Christian centuries / Deborah
F. Sawyer.
p.   cm. – (Religion in the first Christian centuries; 1)
Includes bibliographical references and index.
1. Women and religion–Rome–History.   2. Rome–Religion.
I. Title.   II. Series.
BL815.W6S28   1996
200'.82–dc20   96–2492
                                                          CIP

ISBN 0–415–10748–2 (hbk)
ISBN 0–415–10749–0 (pbk)

For my mother
Margaret Lilburn

CONTENTS

INTRODUCTION

Her face was dark and of a swarthy hue, her eyes were black
and powerful beyond their usual wont, her spirit divinely great,
and her beauty incredible ... her voice was clear and like
that of a man. Her sternness, when necessity demanded, was
that of a tyrant, her clemency, when her sense of right called
for it, that of a good emperor.[1]

Conversely, if the more important, more beneficial concerns
were turned over to the woman, she would go quite mad.[2]

Both these opinions are accurate reflections of their subject and their
time, and yet they are poles apart in their estimation of women's
abilities. Such is the diversity we encounter when exploring the
experiences and understandings of women in the time of Rome's late
Republic and early Empire. In fact, neither 'women' nor 'religion'
should presuppose for us a fixed category. In our own day, and
looking back through history, convincing definitions of what constitutes the female gender, or what constitutes religion have been
elusive, and our contention in this study is that is the way they
should remain.

   Neither experience of religion in our own day, whether of a mass
pilgrimage to Mecca or a papal address at Easter; nor awareness of
issues prevalent in the late twentieth century that affect women, is
going to provide us with working images for our study of life two
millennia ago. An ideal objective position, which would begin with
a blank page, that we could then begin to draw on using all our
available evidence, is impossible to achieve. We are by our nature
subjective individuals who bring to our scholarship all the interests
and prejudices of our own age, our own gender and our own social

and racial realities. In positive terms we can attempt an honest reconstruction that consciously takes into account the biases we are aware of and not only prevents them misinforming our interpretation, but also allows, where possible, for them to enrich our analysis.

When trying to reconstruct the lives of women in historical contexts we are confronted with the perennial problems caused by lack of direct evidence from women themselves. Their history comes to us from men's writings and from the perspective of men. This observation becomes more pervading the further back in history we go, and women are experienced as the mute and passive objects of male thought and action. Ancient historians wishing to reconstruct a women's history are challenged to look beyond the usual annals of history to more unconventional sources that give reflections and glimpses of the lives of women in antiquity. The work of ancient historians who are attempting to reconstruct women's history has challenged assumptions about the extent of our knowledge of the ancient world by showing how fragmentary our picture of the ancient world actually is, not only as regards information about women, but also regarding people belonging to anything other than an elite class, or specific geographical areas.

These constraints have to be borne in mind in any study that is centred on the experience of women. In attempting to overcome them a variety of methodologies for reading the evidence will be employed which includes those developed specifically for reconstructing women's history. For example, reading 'against the grain', here applied to textual evidence, is a method that goes beyond the written statements themselves to ask about the contexts that have prompted them. In the case of prohibitions against women's inclusion in public affairs we would ask why it was thought necessary to have to exclude them. What were they doing to attract such attention?

The difficulties related to depicting women's lives in the ancient world are myriad, and the problems with our particular task are compounded by the context of religion. Here accounts from the ancient world, Greek, Roman, Jewish or Christian, are notoriously male orientated in their world view and their 'other world' view. Using a variety of strategies to interpret our material we can hope at the very least to produce a shadowy reflection of the experience of women in the religions of the Roman Empire. What will appear with little effort is the picture of the status and estimation of women by men in those ancient contexts.

WHAT IS 'WOMAN'?

In focusing on women we must not perpetuate the common contemporary error of universalizing their experience.[3] A wealthy freewoman's lifestyle would not be the same as that of a woman slave who was poor. Furthermore, their religious experiences would be of a different order. These are issues that will be fully discussed in the context of the status of women in the Roman Empire, and, in particular, in relation to Greco-Roman religions, Judaism and Christianity.

Neither in our study do we intend to put on blinkers and isolate one sex for scrutiny. Gender roles develop in relation to one another: either complementarily or hierarchically. It would be impossible to begin to understand one sex while ignoring the other which gave the former its identity through contrast and comparison. Any study of women and religion has to be a study of gender and religion to a greater or lesser degree. Here we do not assume to provide an analysis of men's experience of religion or their roles within a variety of religious expression, or the images of men that have evolved from the religious imagination. Rather, while making the concept of woman our focus, we will articulate factors concerning the other sex as they directly relate to our particular interests, that is, in offering a comparison or measure for the focal point of our analysis. Contemporary debate encourages us to understand gender as a spectrum with clear manifestations of male and female only appearing at the two extremities. Within these extremes people's experience of gender, both through history and within their own lives, ebbs and flows across the spectrum. When we attempt to understand the experience and articulation of what it meant to be a man or a woman in a particular context at a particular time in history, this concept of transgender allows a flexibility in our analysis that is both sensitive to our many and divergent sources, and more plausible than one which presumes that gender categories were ever set in stone.

Mary Beard is one modern commentator who expresses unease about enforcing contemporary categories of 'women' and 'religion' on to an ancient context for which such categorization would be alien. We should not take for granted the existence of a given and accepted concept of 'woman'. Rather gender itself was, and is, an adaptable category: what it meant to be a male or a female in one situation, whether religious or political or social, was open to influence and change from the effect of new or external factors. Mary

Beard puts this point in relation to the categories of women and religion as follows:

> what happens ... if we question the gender category itself, if we see the definition of women and their roles as unfixed, fluid, constantly under debate, never pre-defined? And, more important, what happens if we see religion and religious institutions as one of the most powerful mechanisms used by ancient cultures to negotiate that fluidity, to define 'what it is to be a woman'. .... Gender is constantly being defined within religion; religion and gender are mutually constitutive, not separate poles.[4]

If we analyse the Greco-Roman cults, for example, even at a superficial level, it is apparent that there is not only divergence regarding women's roles among them, but even their beliefs about the nature of women are not uniform. Between Demeter and Isis a whole spectrum of assumptions of what constitutes female experience exists: from passive victims of a society that separates mother from daughter, in the case of Demeter and Persephone, to the all-powerful Isis cult where women would share in the power of transformation, even that which can bring life from death. In the case of the Vestal Virgins we see quite clearly a transcendence of any static concept of women that might be argued to exist in Greco-Roman society.

It is important that we address this issue both in the context of the flux of the pagan Greco-Roman religions at the end of the Republic and the early years of the Empire, and with regard to the religious context of Judaism which was, superficially at least, of a more static nature. If there is a preconceived notion of what it is to be a woman within a given religious context, it might be discernible within Judaism where there is fusion between legislation and belief, a feature that distinguishes it from the Greco-Roman cults. If Judaism cannot provide a clear monolithic definition of the nature and role of female gender, and we might suggest at the outset that diversity is as endemic to the Jewish tradition as it is to the pagan cults, or Greco-Roman myth and legend, then it is left to Christianity to fulfil that expectation. Christianity stands on its own in respect to prescribing the particular roles for men and women, founded on essentialist notions of gender given divine sanction from the moment of the world's creation.

Although the boundaries of our study do not allow us to trespass too far on to the territories of philosophical thought, it would be an artificial and unsatisfying exercise that did not bear in mind the relationship between religious expression and world view. It is undeniable that both Judaism and Christianity developed concepts in dialogue with classical Greek philosophical ideas; and it would be a blinkered scholar who would depict Greco-Roman religion devoid of analogy to contemporary philosophical values and notions. Although the latter category of religion stands in contrast to Judaism and Christianity, being able to flourish without necessarily demonstrating prescriptive moral codes, it does not follow that it was isolated from the influence of such philosophies that were endemic to the very structure and function of Greco-Roman society.

In order to sustain and structure our analysis of the understanding, experience and articulation of what the female gender meant in a variety of mythic and religious contexts in the period of the late Republic and early Empire, we need to offer a theoretical framework to provide a structure for our questions and a measure for our choice of illustrations. By isolating two formative and central classical philosophical notions of gender and applying them as interpretive tools to our traditions and texts, a fusion between thought and ritual, and, by extension, between theory and praxis within ancient society, can be discerned. The scope of our study limits the extent to which we can develop the theoretical dimension of our analysis. Wary of the dangers of oversimplification in this regard, and at the same time aware of the need for brevity, what follows is a basic theoretical framework for our study.

Contemporary gender theory, being formulated across a myriad of academic disciplines, including anthropology, psychology, philosophy, history, sociology, biological sciences,[5] often focuses on the question of whether gender is part of the essence of an individual's identity or instead a combination of conscious and unconscious social and cultural construction. Identifying and applying this focus retrospectively, we discover that Aristotle and Plato provide the same two examples of gender theory: the former offering an essentialist view, the latter one of construction.

In our analysis of the ways in which Christianity understands gender, specifically in terms of the nature of women and the roles they should fulfil, we will discuss Aristotle's notion of natural order which pre-elects a woman's role through recourse to her nature as natural subject. Conversely, the role of men is prescribed in relation

5

to their natural pre-election to rule.[6] This position can be construed as the epitome of gender theories based on difference, the traditional *bête noire* for feminists. Difference between the sexes embodies the central concept of duality that has dominated western civilization.[7] Difference allows for the two extremes on the gender spectrum to be normative for men and women. Difference in the context of patriarchy becomes a means of accounting for women's marginalization in the public sphere, and its focus on the distinctive female role in nature, in child-bearing and nurturing, allows for their exclusion from decision making on rational grounds.

Within Plato's thought there can be discerned the possibility that women should not be excluded from any activity by virtue of their nature.[8] Although, unsurprisingly, there are many passages in the *Laws* which support traditional ancient Greek attitudes to women's station within the seclusion of the domestic realm, it is not at all clear that his thought assumes that by virtue of their nature, or *phusis*, women are essentially inferior to men. Saunders includes *Magnesia* in his analysis of Plato's understanding of women, and does not restrict himself to the utopia of the *Republic*. This is a crucial inclusion since this work describes a state that is 'second-best' to the Republic, and if women are included alongside men by virtue of their ability, then the intention to integrate them into society does not exist merely on the plane of the ideal:

> In the *Republic*, Plato sketched a state positioned at one extreme on the scale of political maturity, in that it was under the untrammelled control of persons acting in the light of advanced metaphysical knowledge of moral values. These persons were, indifferently, men and women. For Plato's policy was functional and pragmatic: women are not essentially or invariably inferior to men in intellect and capacity to rule; therefore let suitable females be chosen as Guardians, on the same terms as males. The incorporation of selected women into political decision making was thus total.

This thinking does not only apply in the context of unrealized intellectual maturity, but also within the organization of a state where more realistic goals are attainable:

> Now in so far as Plato incorporates into the educational structure and the social life of Magnesia not just a female intellectual elite, but *all* citizen women, whatever their intellect,

by means of the provisions regarding the academic and artistic syllabus, the military training and the common meals, he is attempting to express in practical terms, with pragmatic abatements appropriate to a second-best Utopia, the ideal female role and status outlined in the *Republic*.[9]

One way of taking account of both Plato's contemporary misogyny on the one hand,[10] and his enlightened concept of female roles as constructed in the light of, or lack of, education and opportunity on the other, is to see that he allows for both 'difference' or essence *and* construction in terms of gender understanding. When we discussed the concept of a gender spectrum above,[11] although allowing for flexibility in terms of self-definition and social constructs, it also has two clear definitions at each polarity: male and female. Thus the spectrum represents clear difference alongside possibilities for development and change. The significant difference between the thought of Aristotle and Plato is not that one sees women's roles as reflections of their given and essential natures, while the other sees gender roles as flexible social constructions. Although the former may be true of Aristotle, the position of Plato is more complex. Plato recognizes both 'difference' (or polarities), in relation to gender, albeit in pejorative, negative statements about women in relation to men,[12] and also 'construction', that is, the equality of opportunity offered to men and women in his blueprints for government.

Feminist critique in our own day initially worked within the confines of patriarchy. Accepting a clear distinction between the sexes, it focused on reclaiming and making positive the differences that had made women the second sex. Feminism itself created an essentialist concept of women and spoke of 'women's experience' as though there was a commonality of oppression for all women stemming from patriarchal society. Such an overarching critique, so closely mirroring the object of its criticism, soon was itself the object of deconstruction.[13] Feminist theory in the context of postmodernity can move beyond understanding gender in terms of fixed categories. The concept of a spectrum signifying the diversity and complexities of our experience of gender, and with its inclusion of two polarities, allows for the existence of difference without prescriptions for behaviour. Such a working framework for male and female participation in the state is anticipated in the philosophy of Plato. In the context of our present analysis of roles of women and notions of womanhood as they relate to ancient religion, it helps to account for the diversity both in beliefs about women and in the variety of their contributions.

At the beginning of this section we noted a comment by Mary Beard,[14] calling for caution in our use of the categories 'women' and 'religion'. She also asked for awareness of the contribution religion itself makes to the construction of male and female categories. This question will be the particular focus of the last section of this study where we shall look at a variety of 'ideals' of womanhood and the notions of gender offered by Greco-Roman religion, Judaism and Christianity.

'RELIGION' AS A CATEGORY IN THE ANCIENT WORLD

As we have just observed, it is not possible to use the term 'religion' and believe that it conveys one specific meaning for all time. If we take the obvious example of religion in western society, Christianity, and look to the period that is the focus of our study we discover that the equivalent Latin term frequently used was *superstitio*, and not *religio*.[15] The latter term, related in meaning to legislative language, included the meaning of 'obligation' as applied to a devotee's reasonable reverence or fear of the god or gods. The former, *superstitio*, by contrast, described *un*reasonable religious belief.[16] It can be argued that what at one stage constituted the category of 'religion' could change, particularly during this unique period of history where different societies and cultures were constantly re-identifying and redefining themselves anew in the light of new experience and ideas. For instance, a notion of 'salvation' alien to Roman religion in many of its manifestations becomes a distinguishing feature under the influence of oriental cults, such as those of Mithras and Isis, which were imported into Roman cities.

Judaism offers us the example of a religion that not only offers salvation, but also a cohesive and comprehensive legislative code, and the blueprint for a society of a 'holy people'. As a system it is a religion, a culture, a society and a state. Its monotheistic belief and its self-definition as an elect people allow for little compromise or explicit assimilation within the context of the Roman Empire. Such a system is both distinctive and unique in that context, but being defined as a religion, allows us to include it in our study and ensures its enrichment.

Christianity begins its life within our period and offers us the opportunity of investigating the origins of a religious movement which, like Judaism, is still in operation today. As with any new child, this religion bears the inherited marks of its parents as well as the constructs placed upon it by its nurturing environment. The fact that Christianity, though not a significant religion for our period, was destined to become *the* religion of the Empire and, by degrees, of western civilization, prompts us to afford it reasonable space in this study.

WOMEN AND RELIGION IN A PRE-TRADITIONALIZED CONTEXT

Our period of study, approximately from 200 BCE to 200 CE, is distinctive in terms of religious history. It is the time before any single monolithic religion had gained world dominance, that is, it is a time before Christianity. Contemporary commentators use the term 'post-modernity' to describe our experiences at the end of the twentieth century. In contrast to the age of modernity heralded by the Enlightenment, the age of post-modernity challenges and rejects notions of metaphysical truth, or beauty, or reason, or meaning. In such an age monolithic religious systems with truth claims and dogma seem out of place. Such traditional belief systems transform into a series of meta-narratives that deny expression of the self. Structures and institutions that were distinctive of western civilization, particularly in the centuries of modernity, become redundant in the light of post-modern critique.

In the age of post-modernity, women who are disenchanted with the structures and truth claims of Christianity become 'post-Christian'. Marked still by the tradition and yet trespassing beyond its boundaries, these women create their own spiritualities, drawing on their power from 'within' in place of that father-imaged power from 'without'. The phenomena that exist today in terms of individuals and movements that have rejected traditional structures can be termed 'post-traditional'. They bear the scars of the traditions of the past, and yet, as post-modern phenomena, they do not accept the imposition of boundaries to belief or experience.

In recognizing our own age as one that manifests 'post-traditionalization' particularly in relation to religion, would we be justified in describing the period of late antiquity as the time of pre-traditionalization? If such an ascription were to be possible, perhaps we would have a means of understanding that past in the light of our present with less risk of the imposition of an alien set of values or judgements.

Between the contemporary period of post-traditionalization and our historical period of pre-traditionalization, exists the monolithic religious system of Christianity that gave shape and form to western civilization and which serves us with a means of defining traditionalization. The questioning of gender boundaries and a myriad of other religious beliefs and institutions that exist in our own age, is apparent in pre-traditionalization. The acceptance of diversity and also the recognition that there are spectrums of values and beliefs seem normative for western experience *apart* from Christianity, and the imposition of such a monolithic system, when set in relation to both pre-traditionalization and post-traditionalization, can be seen to be artificial rather than organic.

This proposal to set our period in such a broad context that can include even our own inevitably involves oversimplification. In contrast to the period of ancient Rome, our own time bears indelible marks of centuries of Christian influence. Also such an analysis does not allow for the plurality of belief and practice within Christianity itself. In justification of such an oversimplification, I would draw on the innate catholic nature of Christianity that sets as its ideal 'one Lord, one faith, one baptism, one God and Father of all, who is above all and through all and in all' (Ephesians 4.5). Our study will illustrate how alien such a framework was in pre-Christian times, and, perhaps, describe a context that is not so alien to our contemporary world.

Religious experience and belief are addressed in three categories in our study: Greco-Roman, Jewish and Christian. The first part of this book sets out to describe significant features of the Greco-Roman world, Jewish religion and society, and embryonic Christianity which have particular relevance to women. Here although reference is made to Christianity, we have to bear in mind that for the period which concerns us this new religion had not developed a clear socio-political context of its own, and its central characteristics were not distinct from those of the Greco-Roman or Jewish worlds.

In Part II we explore the types of experience women encountered in Greco-Roman religion, Judaism and Christianity; and then in the final part we discuss how women were portrayed in those religious contexts and how the nature of womanhood was understood in relation to men, the deities, and each other. The scope of this study is vast, and it would be impossible to produce a total picture of religious belief and practice in late antiquity. The examples from Greco-Roman religion, Judaism and Christianity have been chosen with care in our attempt to reflect the life and spirit of this diverse and intricate religious world.

Part I

THE SETTING –
ANCIENT GREECE
AND
HELLENIZATION

Significant factors that need to be taken into account in assessing the lives of women living in late antiquity who encountered the religious environments of the Greco-Roman cults, Judaism and Christianity, are many and complex. The intention of this initial part of our study is to bring them to the fore and identify them from the wider categories of Hellenism and ancient Rome, to the more narrow ones of Judaism and Christianity. In this first part we attempt to recreate the atmosphere of women's lives in the ancient world; then to note the distinctiveness of Jewish life for women; and, finally, to begin to understand the content of a new religious movement of that time, Christianity, and what it might have promised to women living in late antiquity.

The pervasive influence of Hellenism left the world with a political, social and cultural heritage, the extent of which has never been surpassed. It would be as impossible to assess the influence of Hellenization on the ancient Roman world as it would be to measure its continued effect on our present age. In order to paint a realistic picture of the time of the Roman Empire, at the very least we need to note the salient features of that Hellenistic, and, in particular, Greek influence, while always bearing in mind that its all-encompassing nature can never be contained within clearly defined boundaries.

Since our preoccupation is with women and religion in the Roman

Empire, Hellenistic influence concerns us here only in so far as its philosophy and beliefs were prescriptive for the status of women at that later time, and influential in the evolution of the Greco-Roman religions, ancient Judaism, and, subsequently, early Christianity.

A general point to note is that as Rome extended her boundaries, taking over greater parts of the Hellenistic world, even Greece itself which was the centre of that former empire, opponents of Hellenistic influence believed this encounter led to the lowering of moral standards and a move away from the simplicity of Roman life. One champion of such a view was Cato, a key figure in Roman politics at the beginning of the second century BCE. However, even he could not escape the pervasiveness of Hellenistic influence, and, ironically, when it came to writing his account of Roman history, *Origines*, Hellenistic traditions were incorporated alongside local legends. In fact the concept of writing an account of origins was itself inspired by Hellenistic models.

Despite the efforts of Cato and others, from the time of the First Punic War (264–241 BCE), the gates of Rome were enthusiastically opened wide to Greek and Hellenistic influences. Hellenism was the emblem of civilization, standing in contrast to the culturally barbaric image of the emerging power of Rome. The influence of Greek culture on Roman life can be traced back to the time of Alexander the Great's Empire when Greek cities were founded on Italian soil. Naples (in Greek, Neapolis – 'new city'), founded by Greek colonists in the sixth century BCE, was a key example. Influence came directly from the continuous influx of Greeks into Italy, particularly from teachers who were often slaves, as well as from traders, craft workers, artists and politicians. The almost total immersion of Rome and large sections of Italy in Greek culture justifies the use of the term Greco-Roman to describe the developing Roman world from at least the third century BCE.

In setting the scene for our observations on the interaction between women and religion in our given period, our intention is to examine religion within its broader social, political and cultural context. The overlap between society and religion both in Judaism and the pagan religions of the Empire will mean that inevitably, even at this early stage, our discussion includes a religious dimension.

Jews like any other people of the ancient world were influenced socially, politically and culturally by Hellenism. This was true for those living in Palestine and those who had settled in the cities throughout the Hellenistic world. Except for the brief period of autonomy following the Maccabean revolt in the second century BCE, the Jews of Palestine had to exist under the Persians, Greeks, Ptolemies, Seleucids and, finally, the Romans. All these powers left their marks on the traditions of Judaism to a greater or lesser extent. The concept of life after death, for example, although articulated in a uniquely Jewish way, belongs to the world of Persian religion.

Greek influence was inevitable from the time of Alexander the Great's extensive empire-wide Hellenization programme in the fourth century BCE. The language of the empire was Greek, as a result innumerable examples of Greek loan words can be found in Hebrew and Aramaic texts, while from the second century BCE religious literature was being written with Greek as the primary language.[17] The Jewish law, the Torah, was translated into Greek to produce the *Septuagint*. A gymnasium was built in every city, including Jerusalem, and, in becoming a member, the opportunities it provided for social, professional and commercial betterment ensured its popularity. The environment of the gymnasia encouraged conformity of style and dress, bringing about assimilation implicitly and subtly. Undressing at the gymnasium exposed the distinctive mark of circumcision, and according to the Jewish writer of *1 Maccabees*, Jews who embraced Hellenism most enthusiastically were prepared to undergo an operation to remove this mark. Assimilation had its critics, but the inviting and beneficial aspects of the new culture meant it succeeded in infiltrating Jewish life. The fruits of Hellenization were tempting and Jewish culture was registering its effects, whether judged as complementary and enriching, or erosive and adulterating.

Greek civilization might have been welcomed as an enriching element to many aspects of Roman culture, but, as we shall see, its social system had little that was positive to offer Roman women. In Greek society the dichotomy between the domestic and public realms meant the strict containment of women's lives. By contrast, in Roman society the dividing line was unclear and many domestic occupations and interests crossed into the public sphere. It would not be unusual, for instance, for a Roman woman to accompany her husband to a dinner party, while in Greek society any women attending such a party would tend to be foreigners engaged for the evening. With this contrast in mind, we begin in the domestic sphere to paint a fuller picture of women's lives in ancient Rome.

1

ANCIENT ROME AND WOMEN'S LIVES

Even a glance at the evidence shows us how far Greek and Hellenistic practices and beliefs led to a submissive and excluding role for women within the domestic sphere, in contrast to Roman society where they are at the heart of domestic life. Aristotle had defined the female sex as defective and the male as normative,[18] and in practice such a philosophy led to men, often slaves, being responsible for the early education of boys rather than their mothers which had been the usual practice in early Roman society. Roman traditions continued alongside newly introduced Greek ideas and practices, however, and this meant that there was variety regarding the estimation and role of women in Roman society.

In the upper echelon of Greek society women who were not slaves and who were married to the head of a household, led lives of seclusion from male company, spending most of their time in the *gynaikonitis*, the women's quarters. Outings from these quarters would almost always be related to religious observances, and therefore did not include other areas of the public sphere such as the market, or the law court, or places of education. Moving down the social ladder, it appears that both sexes mingled more in the public arena where women slaves worked alongside and served men. There was also the category of foreign women, mentioned already, whose role was to provide entertainment: music, dancing, engaging conversation, as well as sexual pleasures for men when they met together outside the domestic sphere.

While according to Greek custom many women lived in almost total seclusion from men both in domestic and public life, a Roman wife would have had a high profile not only in household management where she had the task of overseeing male servants and slaves, but also in the education of both her sons and her daughters.

Legislation from 19/18 BCE provides interesting evidence concerning marriage in early imperial times. At this time there was an attempt to impose on Roman society good family values, as understood and interpreted by the imperial household of Augustus.[19] The central reason for this seems to have been the increasing need for manpower in the Roman legions,[20] since it was felt in certain quarters that Roman society had become dissipated,[21] and that the very existence of family life was threatened by a younger generation who preferred promiscuity to stable relationships. Two laws were passed by Senate. The first was to enforce marriage for men between the ages of 25 and 60, and for women between the ages of 20 and 50; and the second to restrain adulterous behaviour. This legislation was strengthened by a system of incentives; for example, a Roman mother of three children was given autonomy over her property. The same applied to an Italian mother of four, or mothers who had five children from other parts of the Empire. A Roman man who had fathered three children received rapid promotion in his public career; as in the case of mothers more progeny was required to qualify outside of Rome.

Judging from the content of this legislation we can deduce that it could only have been directed at the upper strata of society. Its overriding significance, putting aside the need to feed the constant appetite of the Roman legions, was that it kept inheritances intact and built on them through auspicious marital alliances.[22] Members of the families and households of senators were the most significant group in terms of political power and invested wealth. Next were the equestrians, a grouping who were wealthy but who could only exercise political power indirectly. The legislation had little relevance to the lower classes, that is to say, the stratum of society known as the plebeians. Other Roman legislation on the family would have had limited relevance to the non-wealthy or non-landed classes.

One complication in this apparently clear-cut social system was the position of freed slaves. Although a good number belonged to the plebeian classes, one must remember that many had more in common with equestrian or even senatorial groups since they had belonged and contributed to those households. Many were very well educated and had been responsible for the education of the children of upper-class families.

The basic structure of the Roman family or household revolved around the *paterfamilias*. For upper-class households the position of this male head would be an especially important one since he would control more wealth and have more opportunity to exercise power than he would have in poorer households. Although the same structure applied to the lower classes, the head of a poor family obviously would have had less power. *Paterfamilias* was an officially recognized domestic institution, the basic social unit at every level of Roman society. Any change of headship for a family required a legal decree.

The outward appearance of Roman society, based on this type of family structure, to our modern critical gaze is overtly patriarchal and hierarchical. There would appear to be little room for female liberation. The situation for women was little different from those women in Greek or Hellenistic society. In fact the most ancient forms of Roman marriage held women in total subjection to their husbands as they had been in total subjection to their fathers prior to marriage.[23] But women's discontent at this situation led to the general abandonment of these types of union by the third century BCE in favour of 'free marriage'. In this new system a woman remained attached to her former family, she retained her own property, and she had the freedom to divorce her husband. This was a great achievement for women in the ancient world, a point reflected in a comment by the legal historian Fritz Schulz:

> The classical law of marriage is an imposing, perhaps the most imposing, achievement of the Roman legal genius. For the first time in the history of civilization there appeared a purely humanistic law of marriage, viz. a law founded on a purely humanistic idea of marriage, as being a free and freely dissoluble union of two equal partners for life.[24]

Although such a marriage may be without precedent in the ancient world, it did bring with it attendant problems – as we might expect when such a significant element of female emancipation was introduced into a patriarchal marriage. These problems may be over-represented in our sources since they all reflect the male perspective. For example, at the end of the second century BCE Livy records Metellus Numidicus exhorting men to marry with the following sentiment:

> If, Romans, we could get along without a wife, we would all abstain from this annoyance; but, since nature has arranged things so that we can neither live with them very comfortably nor without them at all, we must look to our lasting well-being rather than the pleasures of the moment.[25]

The context for such a negative view of marriage is to be found in the upper levels of Roman society in the particularly problematic situation of a household that included a rich wife. A husband gaining a rich dowry on marriage was able to use it as he willed, whether to pay off debts or to invest. If his wife then wished to divorce him, and if he was unable to prove her to be morally defective or to be divorcing him without cause, then he would have to return the dowry intact. This type of problem illustrates well the clash between female emancipation and a *paterfamilias* structure. While the husband as supreme head of the household can dispose of its wealth as he deems fit, his power is emasculated when his wife exercises her legal right to be free of him.

We cannot doubt the enlightened nature of this legislation for free marriage in Roman law. What is problematical is its introduction into a continuing patriarchal society. Rather than being an element of reform in that context, such emancipation can fuel undercurrents of prejudice and, in particular, misogyny. For Roman marriage to have been truly liberating for its women the notion of *paterfamilias* would have had to be radically changed.

In order to clarify the position of Roman women, and, by implication, other women living in the Empire under the direct influence of Rome, we need to glance back to earliest times, to the days of the early Republic,[26] and in particular to the law of the Twelve Tables (451–450 BCE). According to this law the position of women throughout their lives is under the control of a male figure. Like that of her brothers, a female child's life was always at the mercy of her father who held the legal right of *ius vitae et necis*, life and death, over his children. He would not be culpable if he murdered his child. In practice this legal right was usually exercised only in relation to selecting which children should be exposed at birth to die, but in theory it applied throughout an offspring's life.

A system of tutelage is outlined in the Twelve Tables which compensates for the death of a father. In this circumstance many of the strict power-controls a father could exercise over his daughter were passed on to a relation on her deceased father's side of the family who became her tutor (*tutor legitimus*). Scholars have pondered this legislation and the implications about the estimation of women that it reflects, and many have concluded that women were believed to be incapable of managing their own affairs.[27]

Unreformed marriage at this time, as we have seen,[28] meant that women passed from the sovereignty of their father to that of their husbands, and in marriage they became *in manu*, 'in the hand of', or 'in the control of' their husbands.[29] Whether this included the right of *ius vitae et necis* is unclear but not impossible.[30] Evans concludes his evidence on the legal status of women during this early period as follows: 'in early Roman society all women, regardless of their age, were in a state of permanent ritual and jural subordination to their husbands, fathers, or guardians.'[31] He notes that the only exception to this generalization was the example of the Vestal Virgins, a group we will be exploring in detail in later chapters.[32]

As we have seen, the development of free marriage in the second century BCE was a significant stage in the emancipation of Roman women.[33] The liberation involved in this type of marriage showed that much of the legislation that had grown up around the archaic forms of marriage was anachronistic and inappropriate, but it took time for Roman law to catch up with actual practice in people's lives. For example, Augustus' legislation towards the end of the first century BCE which was intended to raise the birth rate,[34] led to women being legally free of their guardians, on condition that they bore the required number of children.[35] However, the role of guardian had already become perfunctory, and in practice a woman could change her guardian, by applying to the praetor, if her original one was unaccommodating to her wishes.[36]

Female emancipation in the late Republic and early Empire period certainly enabled women to cultivate and develop interests outside the home, although they always operated from that context. But we must bear in mind that the convention whereby a young woman would move from the household or family of her father to build one for herself and her husband remained static. The concept of a single woman existing outside of a domestic context only crept into the social structure of the Roman world in any discernible way with the emergence of Christianity and the cultivation of the 'celibate woman'. In fact one aim of Augustus' legislation of 19/18 BCE was to ensure that women between the ages of 20 and 50 should be married.[37]

On the other hand, the fact that most women of the nobility were well educated meant that they could enjoy relative freedom and engage in interests beyond domestic concerns. We find indirect references to women's academic achievements in accounts of their sons' education. Agricola's mother educated him in the liberal arts until he was reaching adulthood and prepared him for the role of senator. Likewise Cornelia taught her two sons, as did the mother of Caesar, Aurelia, and Augustus, Atia.[38] These do not refer simply to lessons in early discipline and good manners, but to advanced academic studies as well. Indeed, in the case of relatively wealthy families, the mother's role became increasingly significant as the child approached adolescence and progressed both emotionally and academically. In her study of Roman motherhood, Suzanne Dixon makes this point: 'This probably enhanced the mother's status in the child's eyes, for, like the father, she would become associated particularly with the business of becoming more grown-up and interesting.'[39] It might be inferred from this that women in their early years must have received a similar household tutoring to that which their brothers enjoyed. Although this may have been so in the case of children, a sharp distinction was made between sons and daughters as they approached adulthood. In her chapter on 'The Roman Family' Beryl Rawson comments as follows:

> But from a boy's coming-of-age ceremony he became a citizen in a sense his sister never would be: he would have a vote and could have a public career ahead. It was at this point that the father's influence must have been decisive, and the unequal political roles of men and women thus differentiated the father–son relationship from the father–daughter.[40]

A revealing example of women's emancipation during the period of the late Republic is given by the historian Livy who lived later (between 59 BCE and 17 CE) than the period he recorded.[41] It concerns a debate in the Senate in 195 BCE over the repeal of the Oppian Law, and a notable demonstration by women against this legislation. The *Lex Oppia* had been passed in 215 BCE to deal with a problem that had arisen as a result of the heavy losses inflicted on the Roman military forces by Hannibal in the Second Punic War. Every family was bereaved, according to Livy's account, and when their fathers and brothers were eliminated by Hannibal, women's financial resources increased at a disproportionate rate. The state intervened to rectify this situation by introducing the Oppian Law which put severe restrictions on women's wealth. It forbade women to own more than half an ounce of gold, to wear robes trimmed with purple, or to ride about Rome in two-horse vehicles. This law was in force for twenty years before it was met with extreme resistance. Many felt that by this time it had lost its relevance, and women felt so strongly about the need for change that they protested in the streets of Rome and outside the Senate when the cases for and against its repeal were being heard.

As might be expected, one clear opponent of its repeal was Cato the Elder. The speech he gave to Senate in support of his stance was preserved by Livy,[42] and although the historicity of this record may be questioned,[43] the content is in sympathy with Cato's comments and tone elsewhere. This extract reflects his conservative stance on women's emancipation:

> What they want is complete freedom – or, not to mince words, complete licence. If they carry this present issue by storm, what will they not try next? Just consider the number of regulations imposed in the past to restrain their licence and to subject them to their husbands. Even with these in force, you can still hardly control them. Suppose you allow them to acquire or to extort one right after another, and in the end to achieve complete equality with men, do you think you will find them bearable? Nonsense. Once they have achieved equality, they will be your masters.[44]

Cato's argument was countered by Lucius Valerius, also recorded by Livy, who ridiculed the new legislation: 'You, being a man, can have a purple saddle-cloth; the lady who presides over your household will be forbidden to wear a purple cloak; and so your horse will be better turned out than your wife.'[45] It would be misleading to describe Lucius Valerius as a liberal on the question of women's lives in modern terms since he goes on to argue that marital hierarchy should be characterized by paternalism, although he opposes Cato's model of servitude. But his speech does at least show that there was more than one male view on the subject.

Another display of female solidarity over a particular cause happened in 42 BCE when Hortensia, a nobleman's wife, led a group of some of the wealthiest women in Rome to the Forum to confront the Triumvirate, Anthony, Lepidus and Octavian, over the latter's appropriation of property which, rightfully, belonged to the wives of their enemy.[46]

A constant counter-argument to any such evidence for women's emancipation in ancient Rome recurs in the numerous examples of legislation reflecting the belief that women are morally weak creatures. This goes back to comments in the Twelve Tables, widely believed to be later interpolations from the beginning of the imperial period or later, and to reflect the popularity at that time of Aristotle.[47] Such disdain for female wealth and emancipation is thus often dismissed as a Greek rather than a Roman trait, and when found in

Latin sources thought to be due to Greek influence on the writer. However, as we have seen, Cato in his speech to Senate calls for the preservation of the Oppian Law and he does so as a self-styled upholder of traditional Roman values – not Greek. Another example from his speech displays his abhorrence of female independent wealth:

> 'In order that we may glitter with gold and purple', says one; or 'in order that we may be driven through the city in carriages on festal and working-days, as if in triumph over the conquered and broken law and over your votes, that we have captured and taken away'; finally, 'that there be no limit to our spending, no limit to our luxury.'[48]

Simply because this is similar in tone to Aristotle's condemnation of female inheritance in Sparta,[49] that does not necessarily signify the dependence of Cato on earlier Greek philosophy. For both Aristotle and Cato the politics of their particular times had led to a change in the *status quo* where the tradition of filial inheritance had been overturned. Both voice the reactionary call to return to the practices of former times when male and female roles were clearly distinguished and the boundaries of women's lives, inside the domestic sphere, and under the control of their husbands, were clearly drawn. Whether such a social system was ever universally realized either in ancient Greece or in ancient Rome, remains a matter of debate. The fact that the boundaries had to be clearly reiterated and underlined by recourse to the philosophy of Aristotle, in the case of Greece, and the words of the Twelve Tables in Rome, could actually suggest that, in practice, these lines were not always quite so clear.

When women took advantage of the liberation that came as a result of the repeal of the Oppian legislation, their new-found freedom soon attracted comment:

> apart from the opulence of her own dress and carriage, the baskets, cups and other instruments of sacrifice carried in her train on these notable occasions were all of silver and gold, while the number of household slaves escorting her, both male and female, was correspondingly large.[50]

This comment from Polybius on the behaviour of the noblewoman Amelia, though not particularly censorious in tone, is nevertheless keen to detail such a show of wealth. We find a similar comment from the period of the late Republic where the former senator,

Sallust (86–34 BCE), in his account of the Catilinarian conspiracy, describes Sempronia, the mother of Julius Caesar's assassin, Brutus. Sallust explains that despite her good education and many gifts, she had developed a distorted personality through luxurious living:

> Sempronia, whose numerous outrages would not have disgraced a hardened criminal.
> Well-bred, handsome and with children of her own, she had little of which to complain. She was well-read in Greek literature as well as in Latin; her singing and dancing were rather too professional for a lady, and she had many other accomplishments which made for dissipation.
> Self-restraint and chastity ranked lowest in her scale of values; and it was hard to say which she thought less of squandering, her money or her reputation.
> Often before this she had broken her word, lied to escape a debt, even had a hand in murder; and with no money left to pay for her extravagance, she had gone utterly to the bad. Yet she had a good brain; she wrote verses; she was amusing; and whether in the language of the drawing room or the brothel, she was a good talker, full of wit, even of charm.[51]

Sempronia has been contrasted to Cornelia, the mother of Tiberius and Caius Gracchus a century earlier. Described by an historian of our own time as being among 'women who combined wealth with unquestioned sobriety',[52] she earned such a reputation through her devotion to her sons, as the following anecdote illustrates:

> On one occasion, a Campanian matron whom she was visiting showed her a collection of jewels that, according to Valerius Maximus, were *pulcherrima illius saeculi*. Cornelia refrained from comment, he goes on to say, until her sons returned from school; at that moment, she turned to her hostess and said: 'here are my jewels.'[53]

Cornelia can be judged in a positive light among Rome's wealthy women because, despite her wealth, motherhood is still her overriding preoccupation. This assessment reinforces the notion that a woman's domain is the domestic one, and even if she, personally, has control of wealth and luxury, her true worth is measured in terms of her family.

The implication is that excessive show of wealth is particularly offensive when displayed by a woman, a view expressed in the

Roman sources. When a similar scene features a senator or a man of wealth and stature, it is seen by all but the most conservative senators, who were ceaseless in their condemnation of luxury,[54] as an appropriate display of high rank within Roman society. When trying to fill out the background to the legislation regarding women's emancipation, particularly relating to the Oppian Law, we can take a lead from comments made by Sarah Pomeroy.[55] She notes that it would be to the advantage of powerful men if the women associated with them were able to display great luxury. Thus, though the determined demonstration by women in the streets of Rome may have contributed to the repeal of *Lex Oppia*, it was in the interests of many men to support their cause, and to enable women in their households to reflect their wealth and its luxurious fruits.

Arguments from Roman history, and reflected in Roman law, on the question of women's emancipation, exemplify the problems relating to any attempt to reconstruct women's lives in history. All these accounts have been written by men, both sympathetic and unsympathetic to the women of their day, and inevitably disconnected from women's own perspectives. Repeated stories of women being prone to alcohol abuse, or inclined to commit adultery, vain, seduced by luxury, and characterized by weakness of character, lead one to conclude that women as cognitive creatures were not taken seriously by their male counterparts. One reason for this slant in the evidence is that the accounts that passed down to us through the work of Roman historians and similar sources are often intended as illustrations of legislation and will inevitably paint a negative picture of women.

Furthermore, since what is at stake is often a question of a sizeable dowry or inheritance, the women represented are from the privileged classes: prominent members of senatorial or equestrian households. For example, we have plenty of evidence voicing male reaction to a woman with a sizeable dowry. Plautus the Roman comedy writer, active at the time of the repeal of the Oppian Law, makes the rich wife a key caricature in his plays:

> those ladies of high rank, those shrews with bloated dowries shouting this and ordering that; the women who, with their carriages trimmed in ivory, their *haute couture* and their purple, reduce their husbands to servitude by their prodigality.[56]

What we lack are accounts from women themselves that might create a more realistic and fuller picture and offer alternative explanations for the attitudes and legislation. Moreover, we need to extend our canvas to include the masses of women who belonged to the plebeian classes, freedwomen and female slaves.

When we move away from the accounts of noblewomen to focus on women from the lower strata of society, our information immediately becomes even more scarce, as it does also in regard to their fathers, husbands and sons. Roman history, as it has been passed down to us, is essentially elitist and relates directly to the lives and preoccupations of those with wealth and power. What evidence we do have tends to be indirect, often anecdotal, and always limited.

Education in the Roman state was the responsibility of the family, thus a good education from academic tutors and learned mothers remained the preserve of the wealthy classes. The plebeian classes learned through the received wisdom of their elders and peers. Children were often equipped for life through trade skills passed on to them from their parents. There were exceptions – being a male slave could mean the chance of a good education. Some slave boys belonging to the vast imperial household could expect to be educated at an imperial school and equipped with appropriate management skills. For some male slave children born within a household, there was the opportunity to be educated alongside the master's children. One well-known teacher in Rome during the first century CE was a former slave. Quintus Remmius Palaemon was a *verna*, that is, he was born in a slave family and, therefore, the possession of a household from birth. He was trained as a weaver, but when he was given the responsibility of accompanying the son of the household to school, he acquired academic learning himself. On gaining his freedom he went to Rome and worked as a teacher.[57]

Education of any formal or planned nature bypassed the lives of women from the plebeian classes completely. Obviously there was a great contrast between the lives of women from the plebeian classes who lived in the countryside and those who lived in the cities.[58] The unrelenting demands of the Roman expansionist campaigns meant that the military forces comprised a significant number of able-bodied men from these classes. Thus many women lived as single mothers, and in the country regions this would also involve tending land and livestock single-handed. The daily toil of hard manual labour was accompanied by the constant fear of losing the small piece of land which was their only means of support for themselves and their children. In the case of the rural regions surrounding Rome, the expansion of large estates, the need to farm large areas intensively for a growing urban population, and the tendency to take over large expanses of land for sheep and goat herds, all contributed to the number of smallholdings dwindling and the peasant class itself diminishing during the years of the late Republic and early Empire. Sallust, writing in the middle of the first century BCE, comments:

> the populace was burdened with military service and poverty. While the generals carried off the spoils of war and shared them with a few friends, the parents or small children of the soldiers, if they had a powerful neighbour, were being driven from their homes.[59]

It may not have been such a bleak outlook for all families with smallholdings, especially since in rural areas households were not so focused on the nuclear family, but instead based on the notion of extended family. A woman without a husband at home could find support in terms of manual help from other male and female relations. A woman married to a soldier who survived the battles could experience an abrupt change in her circumstances if he was fortunate enough to be rewarded with a large colonial estate abroad, often measuring many acres, in exchange for his previous half acre in the environs of Rome.

For those whose land was expropriated, often their only option was to go to Rome and try to find employment. This was not an easy task since the slave market was expanding alongside the Empire which meant that paid employment for free members of the plebeian classes grew more and more scarce. Particularly for the many single women widowed by the military campaigns, survival for the first time in an urban environment was hard. Women in all strata of Roman society were not normally trained for any occupation other than domestic tasks. This reality is reflected in passing in an account of rural life painted by Columella, an estate owner who lived in Italy during the middle of the first century CE:

> god has allotted to man the ability to withstand heat and cold, long journeys, and the toils of peace and war – that is to say, agriculture and military service. To woman, however, whom he made unfit for all these matters, he has entrusted the supervision of domestic affairs. Indeed, since he has assigned to this sex the functions of guardianship and care, for this very reason he also made woman more timid than man, recognizing that fear contributes a great deal to scrupulous stewardship.[60]

In the case of women with large households this could mean that managerial skills were more developed than physical ones, but for the majority of women from the rural plebeian classes work in the main consisted of mundane and relentless cleaning jobs, providing food, feeding the family and the animals; and of making material to make clothes.[61]

Employment for women in the cities included hairdressing, massaging and beautification, though most of the women in these jobs were slaves or freedwomen working for a particular household.[62] Slave women could be apprenticed to local craftspeople in order to learn skills that would benefit their owners. There are frequent references in the literature and on inscriptions of trades and crafts, usually aimed at the luxury market, being practised by a family where both husband and wife would be involved.[63] One example from the mid-first century CE is found in Christian literature. Prisca and Aquila, missionaries and founders of house-churches living in Corinth having been exiled from Rome, are both described as tentmakers (Acts 18.1–4). It is interesting to note that three references that mention the couple record Aquila's name before her male partner's (Acts 18.18; Rom. 16.3; 2 Tim. 4.19). These crafts and their accompanying commercial concerns included working with gold-leaf, purple dye, gem stones, gold embroidered garments and ivory.

Female slaves, and many freedwomen who remained attached to their original households, which was a common practice in Rome and the cities of the Empire, engaged in many diverse skills and tasks. Some were assigned to clearly domestic areas of work, such as cleaning, cooking, mending and providing clothes for the household. Some were closely attached to nurturing and rearing their owner's children; from delivering and wet-nursing their charges to early schooling. Others would be assigned to the more public arena of assisting with the particular trade and commerce that supported the household.

More exotic occupations for women of the plebeian classes were to be found in entertainment.[64] We have evidence of female gladiators, especially enjoyed by Nero and Domitian, actors, and dancers, erotic and otherwise. The women in such occupations were often classed as prostitutes.[65] Other occupations that overlapped the category of prostitute included women serving in taverns and restaurants. Evidence from Pompeii includes a female weaver who was also a prostitute, and a fruit seller who doubled as a pimp for two women.[66] It would seem that prostitution was a trade that attracted many women employed in general occupations of buying and selling, particularly if their location was a thriving sea port. The brothel, the most obvious place to find prostitutes and their pimps, was an institution that thrived in the Roman Empire.

Much of the evidence for prostitution comes from Rome itself, which was probably normative for the other cities of the Empire. Very similar evidence comes from Pompeii, and from other more distant corners of the Empire,[67] while ancient Corinth was notorious for the vast array of vices it could offer its citizens and visitors.[68] Graffiti from the brothels themselves together with literary sources that describe them give us clear insights into the working lives of prostitutes.[69] The brothels were buildings with cramped, dirty, windowless cubicles where women had their price inscribed over the doorway. The prices varied, apparently not in proportion to the beauty of the particular woman, but as an indicator of the type of sexual exercise she was willing to perform. As well as the brothels, the streets, marketplaces, public baths, temples, all provided places for prostitutes to practise their trade; and for those buying, there was as much variety on offer as in the brothels. The customers came from all strata of society: slaves, freedmen, freeborn and the nobility.

The profession of prostitute was not the preserve of slaves or freedwomen alone, but included freeborn women. It provided one of the few opportunities for poor women of this section of the plebeian classes to earn a living, and, particularly, it would be the inevitable fate of the many women who migrated to the cities from rural areas on being widowed and dispossessed of their land as consequences of the constant military campaigns. For most women trapped into prostitution as their only means of survival, life was squalid, poor and hopeless with the prospect of further degradation being the only means of increasing their earning power.

This chapter has attempted to give some insights into the lifestyles and expectations of women living at the time of the late Republic and early Empire. As we have seen, evidence is sparse, particularly when we look for material coming from women themselves; and when we look for any clues at all concerning women outside of the elite upper strata of society, our task is particularly difficult. When assessing women's lives in Roman society the overriding factor to take into account is the class system that was in operation. From our limited overview it soon becomes clear that there is not an all-encompassing 'woman's experience'. A noblewoman's power, wealth, education and freedom are a world away from a slave woman's powerlessness, poverty, illiteracy and servitude. Women's experiences and expectations were varied and diverse. The only general comment to make is that no woman was perceived as equal to a man in terms of her worth to the state. The Roman world may have offered a great degree of liberation to women when set in contrast to their role in Greek society, but it was patriarchal to its core: in its legal system, its government and its domestic organization. If women did gain emancipation it would always be limited by these constraints. It would be liberation within a patriarchal structure, rather than liberation from that structure.

2

WOMEN WITHIN JUDAISM AND CHRISTIANITY

Narrowing down within the sphere of Hellenistic influence and the dominion of Rome in late antiquity, our focus settles on Judaism. This was a distinctive culture and society within the ancient world, and as such had particular concerns and practices regarding women. This chapter also provides an opportunity to make initial observations regarding embryonic Christianity as it emerges out of Judaism at this time.

In addressing the phenomenon of Judaism in the Greco-Roman world, we have to begin with an apology since we are going to grant this religion more space than its size or influence at the time of Rome's late Republic and early Empire warrants. There are three reasons for this deliberate distortion of balance: first, the unique quality of its notions and practices among its contemporary belief systems and cults attract note; and, second, its enduring influence down to the present day. Finally, as the parent religion of Christianity it occupies the unique position of having given birth during late antiquity to the subsequent monolithic religion of the Roman Empire.

The context for women living within Jewish society during our period was different from any other society in the Roman world. At this stage in our study we need only identify the nature of the distinctiveness since the implications for women's lives within the Jewish religion will be analysed in more detail in later chapters. In the context of looking at women's practical involvement in religion, when we turn to Judaism we are faced with meagre evidence on which to base our reconstruction. Judaism is a highly complex religion that, during our period, included a cultic system, soteriology, philosophy and a notion of sacred texts that was becoming increasingly central.[70] In later chapters we will observe some clear

32

distinctions between it and Greco-Roman religion where the focus was on cultic ritual, and might, as optional extras, include some other ingredient such as speculation concerning immortality.

Given that sacred texts occupy such a central position within Judaism it might suggest that we possess an array of evidence concerning, for example, women's status and contribution in religious matters. These texts, however, are not suited to providing historical reconstruction. They are religious texts, and their primary aim is to strengthen and inform those who would be holy in the sight of God. Their material is selected, formulated and presented with that primary function in mind. Many practices and beliefs are so infused into the minds of the Judaic believing community that they are not even articulated. Furthermore, although some Jewish biblical texts contain material that may date from a thousand years BCE, its highly influential editing dates in the main from the fifth century BCE and although material exists that dates from our period of the late Roman Republic to the early Empire, most was codified and edited at a later date.[71] It is not in the nature of these texts to provide us with a clear, historical description of daily life for a religious Jewish woman in antiquity. Attempts at reconstructing women's lives within the religious community have to employ devious means even to begin to sketch a credible picture.

When we describe Judaism at any time in its history it soon becomes evident that its religious concerns can never be studied in isolation from the type of culture it purveys.[72] The cornerstone of Judaism is the Torah in the written form, which is the first five books of the Bible. The vast collections of rabbinic sayings make up the Oral Torah (*she b'alpe*) which is contained in the Talmud and midrash. This latter collection contains two types of material, haggadah (the homiletic material), and the halakah (the commandments that must be kept to create a people holy in God's sight).[73] The prescriptions and accounts that make up the Torah, both written and oral, are not narrowly religious, but pervade every aspect of life. There are guidelines for dealing with marriage, murder, animal husbandry, land management, household management, relationships between parents and children, the necessary qualities for leadership. These appear alongside the more overtly theological concerns such as prescriptions on worship, and discussions about issues such as the nature of God, the creation of the world, and the origin of suffering.

This integration of religion with all aspects of life reflects the pre-history of Judaism. It began as a nationalistic movement whose strength lay in the syncretization of politics, society, culture and religion. By linking these and making them interdependent and mutually supportive, the founders of the Israelite state could maintain loyalty among its subjects, commitment in battle, and early confidence in the face of its surrounding, and often hostile, neighbours. Its survival depended on allegiance to the one deity, Yahweh, who appointed the nation's monarch and his successors, whose only temple resided in the capital city next to the king's palace, and whose priesthood was inaugurated in cooperation with the king. This was the legacy of ancient Israel which ensured that in contrast to many societies, ancient and modern, Jewish society always had an essential religious identity. In losing its monarchy and cult through the sixth-century Babylonian campaign, core symbols were lost. However, enough remained to provide the foundation for the Jewish religion. It survived in Palestine and the diaspora during the ascendancy of Hellenistic rulers, and in 63 BCE Palestine became an extension of the Roman Empire during Pompey's Near Eastern campaign.

After the annexation of Judea as a vassal kingdom in 63 BCE, and then as a province under Roman governors from 6 CE,[74] Judaism was a religion of the Roman Empire. During this period the temple in Jerusalem attracted the attention and respect of the Roman rulers.[75] This comment made in the revised edition of Schürer neatly sets the Jerusalem cult in context with the oriental shrines to be found throughout the Empire: 'in a sense, therefore, even the exclusive Temple of Jerusalem became cosmopolitan; in common with the renowned sanctuaries of the Gentiles, it received the homage of the whole world.'[76]

The Jewish religion was granted permission by Rome to continue in its usual practices, and its adherents were allowed the freedom to worship and aspire to live holy lives as they were used to doing. In allowing such privileges to the Jews the Roman authorities were protecting the Jewish communities from such extreme repression as that practised by the Seleucid ruler Antiochus IV which could have led to political instability in the provinces.[77] So it was primarily a pragmatic move that led to the protection of the Jewish religion by the Romans. Both Caesar and Augustus made particular efforts to ensure this toleration.[78] This did not mean, however, acceptance and respect from the general populace. Cicero, for example, describes the Jewish religion as a *barbara superstitio*,[79] and Plutarch associates Jewish ritual with the excesses of the bacchae.[80] The satirist Juvenal ridicules what in Greco-Roman eyes are ridiculous practices: abstaining from pork allows the pigs of Juno unwarranted longevity, and resting on the Sabbath encourages lazy people.[81] The concept of separateness, however, attracted the most indignation and hostility:

> Precisely at the time when through Roman world-wide rule and the levelling effect of Hellenism there was a general tendency for local cultures either to be submerged or to be absorbed in the overall Greco-Roman culture, it must have been felt as doubly frustrating that only the Jews were unwilling to be thought of as taking part in the process of amalgamation.[82]

As a religion in a Greco-Roman context, existing as it did throughout the cities of the Empire as well as the provinces of Galilee and Judea, Judaism was unique. Its central belief was that there was only one God who had created and was in control of the heavens and the earth. This assertion did not reflect a refusal to debate religious beliefs in a wider context. Indeed Judaism attracted and revelled in such dialogue. The work of the Jewish philosopher Philo of Alexandria is fully engaged in open debate between the truth claims and beliefs of Judaism and those of Greek philosophy. Likewise the ancient Jewish historian Josephus writes accounts of his God's salvific actions throughout the history of the world, explaining where necessary the role of pagan leaders and armies in the divine master plan. Both writers are at home writing their accounts in the Greek language, and engaging in what is essentially a debate, whether apologetic or historical, more usually found in a Hellenistic or Roman context.

During the time of Roman domination Judaism was visible to the outside world in three central features: its cultic life; its synagogues; and the distinctive behaviour of its adherents, especially circumcision of male babies, the Sabbath, and the dietary rules governing the preparation and consumption of food and drink.[83]

There were important implications for women resulting from the wider political and social climate that was affecting Judaism during these centuries. One of the main influences of the Hellenistic world on women's lives was an intensification of the dichotomy between private and public worlds. Ancient Israelite religion had reflected an agrarian life and community, and the cities that had existed prior to the sixth century BCE, Jerusalem and Samaria, were not large metropolitan conurbations such as we find in the Hellenistic world and in

Roman times. The ancient law codes and homiletic literature reflect settled agrarian communities that centre on family, animal husbandry and land cultivation. In this context women's lives were occupied with transforming the raw materials from animals and the land into products for use in the household, bearing and nurturing children, and, if appropriate, overseeing the domestic staff. Household and land were inseparable, and so public and private, or domestic, divisions are artificial in this context.

The distinctiveness of Judaism in the Greco-Roman world was symbolized by the practice of male circumcision whereby a Jew could be physically recognized as a Jew, distinct from his non-Jewish neighbours.[84] It could be argued that this practice alone established beyond debate the patriarchal nature of the religion, with its accompanying legislation and social expectations. If the primary sign of a Jew is the mark of circumcision on male genitalia, then Jewish identity for a woman can only be of a secondary nature. This 'hierarchy of identity' is illustrated by the custom of male association with the visible public sphere, and female with the invisible private sphere in the Hellenistic period, and also in Roman times.[85] A Jewish literary work of the second century BCE bears witness to this practice in a discussion of how to deal with a headstrong daughter: 'See that there is no lattice in her room, no spot that overlooks the approaches to the house' (Sirach 42.11b).

Writing in the first century CE the Jewish philosopher Philo of Alexandria describes how the ideal domestic quarters offer degrees of seclusion for women, with the hidden, innermost chambers reserved for unmarried virgins:

> Women are best suited to the indoor life which never strays from the house, within which the middle door is taken by the maidens as their boundary, and the outer door by those who have reached full womanhood.[86]

Women's religious identity was marked by observance of rituals associated with the home, practices that made a home a Jewish home, and which instilled in children from their youngest years their own Jewish identity.[87]

A well-documented attitude to female sexuality that is found both in the ancient texts of Israel and in contemporary Judaism of our own day is the taboo on women's menstrual blood. The legislation that articulates this taboo derives from the same religious context as was the case for all Israelite law, namely, the giving of the law to Moses by God on Mount Sinai, and has direct implications for the regulating of women's lives in society. The biblical law states that the regular menstrual flow results in a woman being unclean for seven days, and the implications of this are as follows:

> and whoever touches her shall be unclean until the evening. And everything upon which she lies during her impurity shall be unclean; everything also upon which she sits shall be unclean. And whoever touches her bed shall wash his clothes, and bathe himself in water, and be unclean until the evening. And whoever touches anything upon which she sits shall wash his clothes, and bathe himself in water, and shall be unclean until the evening; whether it is the bed or anything upon which she sits, when he touches it he shall be unclean until the evening. And if any man lies with her, and her impurity is on him, he shall be unclean seven days; and every bed on which he lies shall be unclean.
>
> (Lev. 15.19–25)

These basic regulations for the menstruant woman were annotated and interpreted down the centuries, dealing with all situations as they arose so that the core 'ideal' could be maintained. In practice these regulations created periods of separation for women, away from their husbands and other male members of family and community. They divided the community by gender, and menstruant women themselves formed a community for the period of menstruation, and at the end of their seven days they went together to the pool for ritual bathing.

There have been many scholars from a variety of disciplines who have attempted to explain this particular taboo. Their explanations explore the area of fertility, for example, showing that this attitude to women's sexuality results in sexual intercourse only taking place when a woman is most likely to conceive. Others link it to taboos relating to blood, and the fear and awe attached to it. The regulations are an attempt to control the frightening forces of nature. Feminist critique of this taboo understands it in the general context of patriarchal control over women, with these detached and explicit regulations condemning women's natural functions and underlining their inferior status, while at the same time implicitly reinforcing the superior nature of men.[88] The phenomenon of developing regulations for menstruant women could be understood as a society's recognition that when women live in close proximity to one another

37

their menstrual cycles conform to one pattern. That is, the regulations are written to deal with a situation that arose for many women at one particular time each month. This would be a direct result of adopting the Hellenistic type of household with its specific women's quarters.[89]

The patriarchal nature of Israelite society can be demonstrated further by comparing the passionate desire to be the parent of a male baby with the disappointment associated with the birth of a female. Examples in the Hebrew Bible of this attitude are numerous both in narrative and legal texts. One story that illustrates the type of extreme action that could be undertaken to ensure the continuity of the male line is that of Lot's daughters. Being without the company of any man other than their father, they conspire to get him drunk and have sexual relations with him in order to 'preserve offspring through our father' (Gen. 19.32). The result of these illicit unions is that both daughters conceive and both bear sons. It is assumed that the reader will understand that the daughters themselves do not count as offspring: only a son could ensure the line.

The disparity from birth between the sexes is underlined in biblical law by the post-birth purification regulations. If a woman gives birth to a son she is deemed unclean as she would be at the time of her menstruation for seven days, and then for a further thirty-three days she is restricted from coming into contact with the temple cult. If the baby is female then both periods of uncleanness are doubled, and the mother and baby's isolation within the home and the wider community is intensified.[90]

Women's lack of autonomy in ancient Israelite society is continued into the Hellenistic period. Women belonged either to their fathers or their husbands, and were given with their dowries to their husbands by their fathers. A woman had to be a virgin when being presented as a wife for the first time. If a man 'damaged' a woman prior to her being given away, he had to pay compensation to her father since he had devalued her. Moreover, her father might have been able to arrange a more profitable marriage for her, and, by implication, for himself. In addition to the compensation, the 'violator' had to marry the woman.[91] The high value given to a woman's virginity denotes that in this society she was numbered among the household's possessions. To damage her would be an act of vandalism or, in taking her as a wife without her father's consent, an act of theft.

Unlawful sex with a woman who was betrothed to another man was severely penalized. Both the man and woman were stoned to death if the evidence pointed to the woman being a willing party to the act, that is, if witnesses could testify that she did not scream out in protest. If there were no witnesses to her protest, or if the act took place in an isolated place where there were no witnesses, then the woman would not be harmed. Here betrothal is counted in the same way as marriage: the woman is the property of her betrothed, to violate her is a mortal offence against another man. The text likens it to murder: 'for this case is like that of a man attacking and murdering his neighbour'.[92]

Her husband as her new possessor has similar legal protection for his goods. If, having trusted her father that he has been given a virgin, he then discovers that she has lost her virginity, the husband can return his 'damaged' goods. We are told that such a woman should be stoned by the men of her own community since she brought shame on Israel by playing the harlot in her father's house.[93] Her virgin status can be proved, we are told, by 'tokens of virginity', that is blood-stained linen preserved from the first night she had sexual relations with her husband. This linen was kept by her father as proof of the unsullied goods he was giving away.[94] If the husband is lying about his new wife being given to him without her virginity, and the 'tokens of virginity' are produced to demonstrate the lie before witnesses, then the husband must pay the father compensation.[95] Again, this reflects the father's primary ownership of his daughter. However, since she has had sexual relations with the husband, she must reside with him: 'he must not put her away all his days.'[96]

The section of Israelite law that we have been scrutinizing above is overtly andocentric, being written entirely from the perspective of the men involved. No room is given for the wishes of the woman to be taken into account. For example, would a woman want to return to the house of a man who had lied about her virginity and, implicitly, who would prefer that she be stoned to death? Likewise legislation pertaining to adultery is understood from the perspective of the wronged husband. The situation where a woman is married to an adulterous man is ignored. Adultery is defined as a sin against the husband. Therefore, where a married man has sexual relations with an unmarried woman the offence is not adultery. If, however, the unmarried woman is still attached to her father's household, rather than being a household slave, or a foreign prostitute, then an offence would have been committed against her father. The penalty for adultery was severe, death for both parties.

In this section describing the context of women in Israelite society we have been using mostly biblical material. This material was codified and edited during and after the sixth-century exilic period. When we look at Jewish texts from the Greco-Roman period, for example *Sirach* or the writings of Philo and Josephus,[97] when Judaism was emerging clearly from its parent ancient Israelite religion, and when the influence of Hellenism was at its most powerful, we do not observe any significant change in attitudes towards women. Hellenistic society reinforced patriarchy, intensifying it with sophisticated philosophical arguments. *Sirach*, a second-century BCE text that is part of Jewish apocryphal literature, illustrates this clearly:

> Do not be ensnared by a woman's beauty, and do not desire a woman for her possessions. There is wrath and impudence and great disgrace when a wife supports her husband. A dejected mind, a gloomy face, and a wounded heart are caused by an evil wife. Drooping hands and weak knees are caused by the wife who does not make her husband happy.
>
> (25.21–23)

The argument here against being a 'kept man' is reminiscent of Aristotelian arguments against female possession of wealth, based on the latter's opposition to matrilinear inheritance in Sparta.[98]

The separation and seclusion of women that was characteristic of Hellenistic society was easily synthesized with Jewish custom, summed up concisely by this quotation from Jewish midrash: 'If God had meant woman to rove, he would have created her out of Adam's foot instead of from his rib' (Gen.R. 18.2).

With its taboos related to menstrual blood and the process of childbirth, separation of the genders was normative practice for Israelite and later Jewish societies. Both Hellenism and Judaism were essentially patriarchal in theory and practice, and both shared similar fears and assumptions concerning women's nature, and, in particular, their sexuality.[99] Far greater divergence and variety can be discerned regarding ideas about the nature and roles of women when Judaism and Roman civilization come together.[100] It is when we come to study the available evidence for women's practical participation in temple and synagogue, and some of the narrative material, that an alternative picture begins to emerge, challenging that created by legislation and tradition.

In our analysis of Judaism as a religious phenomenon in the Greco-Roman world we noted that it was a small pin on a large and intricate map of religious experience in the ancient world. One inadvertent contribution Judaism made was to provide a seedbed for a new religious movement to grow, namely Christianity. Christianity merits the space that has been awarded it in this study because of its subsequent history rather than its size or status during the time of Rome's late Republic and early Empire. In the light of later developments in the territories of the Roman world this religion demands attention be given to its formative years. Moreover, Christianity has been the most dominant religious, social, political and cultural influence on women's lives in the history of western civilization. Its influence begins in the mid-first century CE where it appeared in the context of early Judaism. Christianity eventually was to become the most dominant feature of the Roman world. All subsequent dominant powers in those territories and beyond, from the time of Emperor Constantine's conversion until modern historical times, need to be explained to a greater or lesser extent in relation to Christianity. Christianity's understanding of the nature and role of men and women has been the single most influential ingredient in the construction of gender roles and behaviour in western society and its dominions. We will focus on this question directly when we come to address the issue of the nature and construction of gender within religious traditions in the Greco-Roman world.[101] At this point we need briefly to identify Christianity's character and significance as it emerged in the first century to be able to assess, in later chapters, the extent and nature of its contribution to women's lives.

One distinctive feature of Christianity that has to be taken into account is that this religion was actually born during the period of the Roman Empire we are investigating. Although we will argue that it is not recognized, and nor does it identify itself as an independent religion until half a century at least from the birth of its founder, the events that ultimately led to the existence of the most influential religion the world has witnessed, comparable only in later centuries to the rise of Islam, occurred with the birth of Jesus of Nazareth at the beginning of the first century CE. Therefore, unlike the religions we have been discussing up to now, religious practices that are essentially Christian, as opposed to Jewish, were new phenomena to the Roman world. We can argue, then, that Christianity is a religion of the Empire: born in its midst, and destined to determine the identity of that Empire itself in the course of three centuries.

As a religion founded, according to belief, by the Messiah, the Son of God, taking human form in about the year 6 CE, Christianity is recognized as an historical religion, based on a particular event in history. All subsequent doctrinal, ritual and homiletical developments are grounded in that historical moment. Because this historical perspective is so crucial to understanding and analysing Christianity in its early years, an historical framework is perhaps the most useful way to begin.

As a new religious movement,[102] it developed its own identity over and against its parent religion, Judaism, at a rapid rate. During its earliest stage, which is arguably called the Jesus movement, to 70 CE, it would be incorrect to classify Christianity as an independent 'new religious movement', so close is its relationship to Judaism. Rather it is a Jewish 'renewal movement'. It is only at the end of the first century, as both Judaism and Christianity define themselves over and against one another, that we can talk confidently in terms of a new religion, albeit still with close ties to its parent. In our study of women and religion we have to be aware of each stage in that early development in order to analyse the effect each one had on Christianity's perception of women. Attitudes to women that developed in these early centuries became the definitive attitudes for the western world up to the present day. At the beginning of the first century Christianity did not exist, but by the end of the second it had a fixed canon of scripture and a clear concept of orthodox belief and practice underpinned with a theological basis for its understanding and treatment of women.

Christianity begins its existence mid-point in our historical focus with the ministry of its founding figure, Jesus of Nazareth.[103] In essence it begins as a Jewish renewal movement with a millenarian type world view. For Jesus of Nazareth it meant that he saw himself as a vital instrument or key figure in preaching the imminence of the end of the present period of history and the dawn of the next: 'Jesus came to Galilee, proclaiming the good news of God, and saying, "The time is fulfilled, and the kingdom of God has come near; repent and believe in the good news"' (Mk 1. 14–15).

Jesus saw his role at least as the prophet heralding the end-time, or the eschaton, and at most as the Messiah whose tasks will include the defeat of God's enemies in the near future. For his followers, in the light of his death on the cross and their subsequent conviction that he had been raised from the dead, Jesus was not only the Messiah potentially, but they believed he would complete his messianic function in the near future when he would come down from God's right hand in heaven and fulfil God's plan, beginning with the destruction of the ungodly powers:

But in fact Christ has been raised from the dead, the first fruits of those who have died ... for as all die in Adam, so all will be made alive in Christ. But each in his own order: Christ the first fruits, then at his coming those who belong to Christ. Then comes the end, when he hands over the kingdom to God the Father, after he has destroyed every ruler and every authority and power. For he must reign until he has put all his enemies under his feet.

(1 Cor. 15.20–25)

Here we can see how the earliest Christian commentator, St Paul, adapted a Jewish messianic world view to the experience of the death and resurrection of Jesus.

In situating earliest Christianity in its Jewish context, the use made of apocalyptic eschatology is not a surprising discovery since the belief that the Messiah had appeared and that final judgement was imminent meant that apocalyptic-style imagery was a useful resource for the early commentators. From the evidence we have of this messianic movement's relationship with the Roman authorities before 70 CE, in terms of its persecution, it would seem that such imagery would be particularly apposite with its in-built explanation for suffering. The time when Nero was Emperor was a distressing time for the early Christians. According to the Roman historian Tacitus (*Annals*, 15.44), in the early sixties CE they were blamed for the fire of Rome, and it was that context, many scholars believe, which produced the first extant Christian apocalyptic text, the *Book of Revelation*. The earliest stages in the development of Christianity, before 70 CE, do not distinguish it from its parent religion. What can be said concerning Judaism in the Greco-Roman world of late antiquity applies also to Christianity. In fact to Roman eyes Judaism and Christianity were indistinguishable for most of the first century.[104]

When we move to the next stage in the development of Christianity, from its origins in Judea and Galilee as the Jesus movement to its presence in the cities of the Greco-Roman world, which is witnessed to in the Pauline correspondence, we find that the issue of relations with the 'pagan' environment is more evident. A self-consciousness is discernible and there is concern about how a Christian community appears to those outside it, manifested in terms of a need for modesty and decorum. On the other hand, there are fears that the standards and beliefs of that 'pagan' world will infiltrate

43

and corrupt the community. Paul's correspondence to the Christian community in Corinth in the middle of the first century CE illustrates both of these characteristics: 'So, my friends, be eager to prophesy, and do not forbid speaking in tongues;[105] but all things should be done decently and in order' (1 Cor. 14.39–40); and: 'It is actually reported that there is sexual immorality among you, and of a kind that is not found even among pagans; for a man is living with his father's wife' (1 Cor. 5.1).

From the time of the earliest post-resurrection period of Christianity there is evidence of Gentiles converting to the communities. When we note the teaching of Paul in relation to Gentile admission to Christian communities in the mid-first century CE, obvious converts to his communities would be the God-fearers. We will mention this group later when discussing the question of Jewish proselytizing in the Roman Empire.[106] God-fearers were non-Jews who were attracted by Jewish beliefs and customs, but reluctant to undergo the conversion rites. In the case of male would-be converts, this would have been particularly testing since they would have to be circumcised. The God-fearers could take upon themselves as much or as little of the religious demands as they wished:

> There is clear evidence that in the Hellenistic–Roman period a large number of Gentiles, who attached themselves more or less closely to Jewish communities, took part in the Jewish divine service and observed Jewish precepts sometimes more, sometimes less completely.[107]

For these God-fearers Pauline Christianity offered a viable option: full membership without circumcision with many of the attractions of Judaism. From the time of the separation of Judaism and Christianity, by the end of the first century CE, converts to Christianity were predominantly non-Jewish, and as it entered the second century Christianity was an independent religion of the Greco-Roman world.

The vast majority of the evidence we have for Christianity exists in the form of confessional material. We have Christian scripture, that is a list, or *canon*, of texts that have been accepted by the religion itself, which share the common aims of trying to either prompt or strengthen faith in the manifesto of that religion. This characteristic has to be borne in mind when attempting to access the biblical material; to treat these texts primarily as historical information would be hermeneutically unsound. If we are not sensitive to the primary interests and beliefs of the writers, we will fail to understand them correctly. If we can equip ourselves with knowledge of their concerns we will then be in a position to make credible comments on their presentation of events and ideas.

Along with a careful reading of Christian scripture, all of which, except perhaps the second letter of Peter, was produced by the end of the first century,[108] the rest of our evidence comes from comments of Roman historians, and some inscriptions. Among the texts there is evidence to which we can apply sociological criteria for discovering the social structure of the early communities, and the social status of individuals within them. Here the names of individuals have proved to be a fruitful resource. The sociological questions posed in more recent years have been particularly useful in ascertaining a realistic picture of women's functions within the early Christian communities. Here the seminal work of Elizabeth Schüssler Fiorenza has made a contribution to our knowledge in a manner comparable to that of Bernadette Brooten in the field of early Jewish studies.[109] Fiorenza has been instrumental in presenting challenging new interpretations of our sources by raising new questions in the debate on the reconstruction of Christian origins.

Fiorenza's attempt to translate her reconstruction of women's participation in early Christianity to our contemporary situation is the point where she has attracted negative criticism. Daphne Hampson has been strongly opposed to Fiorenza's conclusions, arguing against what she sees as an anachronistic and unrealistic application.[110] Fiorenza's work will be invaluable to us, however, when we look both at the practical nature of women's participation in the Christian communities in the first century and then later when we analyse the notions concerning women's nature in Christian theology.[111]

Two distinct influences encroached upon the position of women in the period of late antiquity; one was the long-standing traditions of the Hellenistic world, and the other was the evolving situation of Roman society. These two currents mark and distinguish tendencies within Jewish and Christian communities, ensuring divergence and plurality throughout our period regarding notions of womanhood and the actual lives of women. This observation leads us into the core of our present study.

Part II

WOMEN IN NARRATIVE AND RELIGIOUS PRACTICE

In the first part of this study we described a diversity of contexts for women's lives during the period of the late Republic and early Empire. In Part II our focus is sharpened and fixed on the types of religious experience expected for and pursued by women at that time. During this period of pluralism poetry, myth, legend, philosophy, sacrifice and ritual from the four corners of the Empire contributed to the vast array of knowledge, speculation and spirituality available to men and women of the ancient cities. This was before the major process of christianization in the Roman world had begun. In terms of religious practice and belief this was a time of adventure and experiment for both men and women. When we examine some key examples from Greco-Roman cults we can imagine the excitement for the citizens of Rome generated by the importation of exotic cults such as Cybele and Attis, or Isis, or Mithras, or Dionysus. All these cults invited initiates to explore and identify with ancient myths of sex and sexuality, of life and death. Within the diversity of the Greco-Roman imagination and spiritual dimension, questions related to the meaning and function of gender identity float naturally to the surface.

By contrast, Judaism would seem to have existed within the ancient cities as an antidote to such extravagant excesses, offering instead of a convincing moral code, a family way of life, and the protection of the one god and creator of the universe. On closer examination, however, diversity was not alien to Judaism during this period, neither in terms of religious practice nor in regard to gender roles. A dissonance can be discerned between the written codes concerning women's lives, and the evidence we have of the actual practices at the time .

It is during our period also that Christianity emerges as a religion distinct from its Jewish roots. Although insignificant in importance in the wider context of the Empire during its first centuries, in the light of subsequent history it is vital to understand the religious foundation of its concepts concerning roles played by men and women, publicly and privately, in any debate involving gender theory and western civilization.

By selecting representative examples from Greco-Roman myths and cults, Judaism, and embryonic Christianity, we hope to paint a picture of the array of possibilities for women's spirituality in late antiquity, and in doing so to reflect further upon the central issues governing women's lives described in the first part of this study.

3

THE GRECO-ROMAN
IMAGINATION

Many of the vast array of religious beliefs and practices evident in the Roman Empire had been inherited from ancient civilizations, and these had been adapted to changing contexts down the centuries. The long relationship of intermingling between the Greek and Roman worlds meant that religious ideas migrated freely, informing and developing indigenous belief systems. The geographical area of Palestine is a pertinent illustration of how religious practice in a particular place adapted to changing circumstances.

In ancient times Palestine was known as Canaan, and its deities, such as El, Baal, Astarte and Asherah, were subsumed into the cult of Yahweh through the dominance of the invading Israelites. The Canaanite cults continued to exert influence and attract adherents despite the dominance of the cult of Yahweh. Some centuries on, faced with the irresistible ideas and practices of the Greek world, Yahwism can be seen to change and adapt again. The concept of written scripture, a belief in the resurrection of the dead and a developed angel and demon cosmology influenced Palestinian religion which can be recognized as rabbinic Judaism by the end of the first century CE. In Palestinian as in other cities of the Roman Empire, religious cults and belief systems from all known corners of the ancient world found expression and support from populaces that were similarly cosmopolitan and, importantly, both curious and adventurous concerning what was often for them a new religious movement.

The dominance of Christianity in western society from the fourth century CE has meant that our understanding of what religion is has been shaped for centuries by that one example. Christianity contains within it not only religious rites such as baptism and eucharist, but also a vast array of beliefs. We can observe a clear distinction between

Christianity and religion in the Greek and Roman context. Christians were defined by what they believed in the first instance rather than by which rites they practised, and, indeed, the latter are usually defined by the nature of the former. In the cults of the Greco-Roman world belief systems were not a central issue. The gods and goddesses were capable of certain actions, often ones that had catastrophic implications for the lives of mortals, for example causing floods, storms or famine. Such gods needed to be placated through offerings of food and drink, or by the sight of beautiful activities such as dancing or music. The climate of Greco-Roman religion is neatly summed up by Dowden in his study of religion and the Romans:

> Most Romans (and inhabitants of the provinces too) were engaged, in their varying local ways, in maintaining the *pax deorum*, by correct observance of rituals at important points in the year and in their lives, and strove to give the gods the honour due to them. They were unworried by souls and afterlives (except that the dead needed placation), reckoned their moral behaviour was up to them and what others thought of them, and had no notion that they needed to be 'saved' from anything – other than bad harvests, disease and childlessness.[112]

Religion in that context did not demand a complex belief system or philosophy. Philosophy was a discipline that existed apart from the deities and their myths and rites, and often discussed notions of God, the role of a divine principle and the like. There is evidence, however, that philosophy and religion, as understood in Greco-Roman terms, did begin to fuse at the beginning of the Empire, apart from Christianity. The oriental cults were usually appropriated by the civic authorities who used their processions for political propaganda purposes, but this was not true of the cult of Mithras.

The cult of Mithras, originally from Persia, but increasingly popular throughout the Roman world from the Hellenistic period onwards, was not characterized by festival processions. According to Richard Gordon, 'the major objective of this cult lay in the provision of religious truth through asceticism and through knowledge of the heavens understood as a veil or screen of truth.'[113] Gordon argues that the central image of this cult, the killing of the bull by Mithras, is in some sense a reference to, and rejection of, civic animal sacrifices. Thus it would seem that a need to breach the dichotomy between philosophy and religion was felt in at least one religion by the first century CE. A further illustration of this is

Christianity, a religious movement that claimed, from the time of its apostle Paul in the mid-first century CE, to provide a system of belief and practice that was equal to and greater than any cult or philosophy available in the Greco-Roman world. It may be significant that both Mithraism and Christianity had many eager converts at the same time. A third 'foreign' religion worth comparing with Mithraism is the cult of Isis which had a distinctive, although not exclusive, female following. Like Mithraism, the cult and myth of Isis included a perspective that looked beyond mundane existence and explored the notion of immortality with the resurrection of Osiris.[114]

Fascinating though the fusing of religion with thought might be, the subject of our study is not philosophy, and any mention of Greco-Roman thought as it evolved through our period is peripheral and relevant only in so far as it can be seen to shape notions of gender or women's lives in a religious context. This will become apparent, for example, when we discuss the philosophical influences on Christian understanding of the nature of women and sexuality. In that context we shall argue that awareness of the philosophies of the Greco-Roman world is vital if we are to understand how women's roles were perceived in that all-encompassing religious belief system.[115]

In discussing Greco-Roman religious practices, by contrast, philosophy is far less central, although it would be a mistake to underestimate the power and influence of philosophy on Greco-Roman life in general. Only the intellectual elite were engaged in developing and debating philosophical issues, but naturally they were the ones who did control the lives and lifestyles of the majority. Philosophy was an essential ingredient of the curriculum in the education of aristocrats and emperors, and it could, literally, lay the foundations of cities, through architectural realization and formalization of notions of order and organization within society. If our study were a comprehensive analysis of all aspects of women's lives in the period of the late Republic and early Empire, then philosophy would be a central concern. As it is, our interest in philosophy is limited to occasional comments on the role played by the philosophical ideas of Aristotle and Plato in the history of religious perceptions of women.

Ancient Greek religions which, in all their rich variety, were a feature of the Hellenistic world, were readily accepted and adapted by citizens throughout the Roman world. It is vital to take account of the whole spectrum of Greek religion since that was in many respects the most important influence on the Roman world during the time of the late Republic and early Empire. In fact the example of Greek religion had already been a reality in Italy from earliest times through the presence of Greek colonial cities like Naples. In the later process of translating varieties of Greek religion into Roman practice, the deities were often renamed, and the religion itself changed to meet new needs.

In this process the role and status of those in power were extremely significant. This situation reflects the integration between the cults and every level of political structure.[116] Often issues relating to the wealth and power of individuals had affected their position within a cultic priesthood, where, for example, their financial contributions to the cult and the often elaborate and expensive rites associated with it ensured its continuance. In this type of situation such priests or priestesses of the cult would be granted favours that lay in the province of the local, regional or even imperial officers. The favour of the gods was vital to those who held political power, and the fun and extravagance of the many and varied rites of the pagan cults ensured the popularity of the government that supported them. The mutual benefits that accrued from the close relationship between the cults and the political governing bodies and the extent to which the cults were manipulated to serve the interests of the wider Empire cannot be overestimated:

> Insofar as there is an overall development discernible in the complex history of the civic priesthood in the Principate, its rationale surely lies in this fusion of the religious system with the socio-political system, a fusion which served to veil from the central and local elites the true character of their domination.[117]

It is clear that women were involved at every level within these cults, from cleaning up the temples to performing the most sacred rites. The attraction of one particular cult over another would depend on a number of variables, such as geographical location, the interests of friends and relations, and financial investment. But one feature common to these cults was the sheer variety of deities and accompanying myths, enacted through ritual, which reflected the whole gamut of human emotion and experience; from the abduction of a child or spouse and sibling rivalry to sexual love and bereavement. One area for exploration must therefore be the locus where these enactments met with the experiences of women living in that time. To what extent could such beliefs confirm and support their lives?

Before addressing Greek religious devotions directly and accessing the extent and meaning of women's participation in them, we need to take a wider look at the thought world of ancient Greece in so far as it continued to inform and instruct Greco-Roman society down the centuries. As we noted in the last chapter, within Greek society women were restricted to the domestic sphere, and their lives can be contrasted to the experiences of women in Roman cities where public society granted them more inclusion and freedom of movement. The process of adopting Greek religion in Rome was explicitly recognized during our period and would regularly occur, during the time of the late Republic, through instruction from the Senate.[118] *IIviri Sacris Faciundis*, the rite for introducing a new type of Greek religion, involved the appropriate persons (*IIviri*) consulting the Sybilline Oracles, so called because they were written, according to legend, by one of the Sybils, prophetesses of Apollo, who lived at Cumae near Naples. Each time new gods and their rites were introduced a particular rite, *ritus Graecus*, was performed. This action was usually prompted by a time of crisis such as a major military campaign or a natural disaster. These oracles continued to be consulted during the time of the Empire, and were only discontinued in 400 CE, by which time Christianity had imposed its own monolithic and uniform system of religious belief and practice on the whole Empire. Then the books were burned.

An illustration of the practice of consulting the oracles is given in Livy:

> By decree of the Senate, the Sybylline Books were consulted. The *IIviri Sacris Faciundis* then for the first time in the city of Rome held a *lectisternium*: for eight days they placated Apollo and Latona, Hercules and Diana, Mercury and Neptune – with three couches (*lecti*) laid out (*strati*) as richly as could be prepared at that time. This rite was also celebrated by the general public. Throughout the city, doors were open and all manner of things were made freely available at the house fronts; everywhere arrivals, known and unknown, were taken off and treated to hospitality, and kindly and affable conversation was held even with enemies. People refrained from quarrels and lawsuits. Even prisoners had their chains taken off for this period – and subsequently it was not felt right to enchain those to whom the gods had brought this assistance.
>
> (Livy 5.13.5–8)[119]

This practice should be set beside the continuing unconscious absorption of Greek ideas and religion that occurred as a result of the two cultures living side by side, from the original Greek colonization of southern Italy, to the later expansion of the Roman Empire. But the display of consulting the oracles does illustrate how Rome publicly acknowledged its debt to Greece.

Despite the fusion of Greek and Roman beliefs and customs throughout the history of the classical world distinctions remained, and one of these, as we saw, was the contrast between Greek and Roman attitudes to women. We noted previously that in Greek society women were expected to remain within the domestic sphere, in subservience to their fathers or husbands,[120] while in Rome the situation was somewhat less patriarchal. We shall now examine some influential myths and legends which may suggest the situation may have been more complex.

The Greek myth of the Amazonian women, if, like other myths, it functioned to reinforce the society that produced it, would seem then to contradict one general presumption concerning the lives of Greek women. It is about women who reject marriage and the confines of domesticity. It describes a society that prefers matrilinear descent to patrilinear, and a society where liberated women even engaged in active warfare.[121] In its earliest forms the myth might have functioned as a mirror of a pre-classical society. For instance, in the Archaic epic of the sixth century the Amazons are described as female warriors who, with their Queen Penthesilea, who was killed by Achilles, battled against Bellerophon and Heracles. But the status of the Amazon stories clearly changed by the fifth century: now they begin to fulfil a role within Athenian society of representing an inversion of the natural and preferred status of women. The Amazon women are now depicted as the female counterparts of the centaurs, the mythical bestial and violent rapists, prompting this comment from a recent collaborative study of women in the classical world: 'Just as centaurs embodied masculinity out of control . . . the violent, promiscuous, and war loving Amazons became an analogous female challenge to the order of civilization.'[122] Their representations in later centuries depict how alien such ideas would be to the patriarchal nature of Greek society. They are said to live in a totally female society, only venturing out for sex so that they can conceive children. Only female babies are welcome; male offspring are offered for adoption or castrated or even killed. Diodorus, writing in the first century BCE describes how Amazon men behave like women tending home and children, and cultivating women's skills such as weaving.[123] The Amazonians are thus held up as the antithesis to Athenian society in such satirical ironic versions of the myth.[124]

Another counter-example to the norm of Hellenistic expectations of women comes from the Greek city state of Sparta where there is evidence, of varying reliability, for an alternative to patriarchal society that lasted from the seventh to the second century BCE.[125] This is important for our study, not least because it sparked a strong and negative reaction from Aristotle whose comments on this particular topic were later taken as a general informed comment on the universal position of women especially within Christianity.[126] Sparta provides the only evidence in Greek society for education being offered to girls on the same basis as boys. The curriculum included athletics, for example, where the girls stripped off as many of their garments as boys did. This would not have been possible outside Sparta and it has been argued that, like the Amazons, Spartan women were used by Aristotle as the 'other' in relation to Athenian women.[127] Their freedom of movement and ease in conversation with men served as a sharp contrast to the usual secluded lifestyle of other Greek women. Added to this, in Spartan law women were entitled to own land and inherit and manage their own property. It is this last feature of the Spartan system that attracted the critical comments of Aristotle who actually argues that this practice was responsible for the decline of that city state's power.

The Lycurgan reform of Sparta that led in the seventh century BCE to the type of emancipation for women so loathed by Aristotle can easily be deconstructed by any far-reaching feminist critique. The main concern of Lycurgus' radical political and societal changes, according to Xenophon's account, was to produce women, fit and well educated, who in turn would produce the most proficient male warriors. For example, in limiting a young man's access to his new wife for sexual relations, the aim was not for the protection of the woman, but to ensure powerful offspring: 'With this restriction on intercourse the desire of the one for the other must necessarily be increased, and their offspring was bound to be more vigorous than if they were surfeited with one another' (*Constitution of the Lacedaemonians* 1.2–10).[128]

The somewhat more enlightened neo-platonist Plutarch was reluctant to blame Sparta's decline solely on female emancipation.[129] On the other hand Aristotle's pessimism regarding any contribution women could have made to Spartan society appears in such comments as 'the licence of the Spartan women hinders the attainment of the aims of the constitution and the realization of the good of the people' (*Politics* 2.6.5).[130] Seeing Aristotle's comments on women as originally applied to one particular historical example of an alternative to an overtly patriarchal society should help contemporary scholars, including theologians, to question the traditional application of his views to the nature of women for all time.

Another example of a divergent articulation on women's nature and experience in ancient Greek society is the figure of Sappho. She was a lyric poet of the seventh century BCE whose work represents a unique female voice that implicitly relates the concerns and interests of a group of women. Often studied with Sappho are the *Partheneia* (maiden songs) of the Spartan poet Alcman. Both provide insights into the feelings and social expectations of women in the Archaic period. They are particularly helpful in detailing the emotional journey from maidenhood to womanhood. One reassuring feature in their literature is the importance of the individual relationships between young women about to enter the married state and older women. The latter acted as mentors and role models for the former, educating the girls in the skills of noblewomen: singing, dancing, performing religious rites and so on.

A particular aspect of these relationships was the development of sexual feelings and actions, reflecting similar male homosexual relationships so common in Greek society and culture. In the case of women, the older partner would seem to be initiating the younger into sexual activity that could be adapted and applied in the marriage bed. The mentor/pupil same-sex relationship would have provided a safe and secure environment for such knowledge to be acquired and practised. Sappho was associated with the cult of Aphrodite, maybe even as a priestess, and the circle of older and younger women that surrounded her on Lesbos practised the rites of that goddess.[131] The *Partheneia* and many of Sappho's poems are characterized by descriptions of relationships that are tender and loving, invoking images from the beauties of the natural world to illustrate the intensity of feeling:

> Hither to me from Crete, to this holy
> temple, where your lovely grove
> of apple trees is, and the altars
> smoke with frankincense.

Herein cold water rushes through
apple boughs, and the whole place is shaded
with roses, and sleep comes down
from rustling leaves.

Herein a meadow where horses graze
blooms with spring flowers, and the winds
blow gently . . .

Here, O Cyprian, taking [garlands],
in golden cups gently pour forth
nectar mingled together with our festivities
Fragmentary Poem 2[132]

As we shall see in the next chapter when we discuss the relationship between Demeter and Persephone, the progression from maiden-hood to womanhood in Greek society was scarred by the pain of separation. When she is given by her father to the husband he has chosen for her a young woman has to leave the close and loving relationship of her mothers and sisters, and other female companions with whom she has lived in seclusion all her life, to begin a new life, often with people she has never met, in a place she has never visited. Sappho's poetry marks these tragic separations:

'Honestly, I wish I were dead!'
Weeping many tears she left me,

Saying this as well:
'Oh, what dreadful things happened to us,
Sappho! I don't want to leave you!'

I answered her:
'Go with my blessings and remember me,
for you know how we cherished you.

'But if you have [forgotten], I want
to remind you . . .
of the beautiful things that happened to us:

'Close by my side you put around yourself
[many wreaths] of violets and roses and saffron . . .

'And many woven garlands
made from flowers . . .
around your tender neck,

'and . . . with costly royal
myrrh
you anointed . . .

'And on a soft bed
. . . tender . . .
you satisfied your desire . . .

'Nor was there any . . .
nor any holy . . .
from which we were away,

. . . nor grove'
Fragmentary Poem 94[133]

The examples of Amazons, Spartan women and Sappho, in different ways, give us glimpses of alternatives to the usual depictions of women's lives in the Hellenistic world. They show us that there was a variety of ways to construct gender roles or to understand the nature of women and men. This evidence of diversity in the ancient world, even found in the time of Aristotle, makes the later Christian attempt to impose universal concepts of manhood and womanhood incongruous.

4

GODS AND GODDESSES

One goddess cult of ancient Greece that belonged to the great mystery religions, and was particularly popular with women, though not exclusively so, was that of Demeter. The mysteries of this great cult were celebrated by Athenians at Eleusis as well as in the ancient Greek colonies of, for example, Sicily and southern Italy. This religion remained limited, in the main, to the religious experience of Greeks and Greek colonists possibly because the central myth and ritual of the cult reflected so closely the lives and expectations of women in Greek society. This feature is illustrated by the Homeric *Hymn to Demeter* composed most probably in the later seventh or early sixth century BCE at Eleusis which describes a young girl's journey from puberty to womanhood.

The hymn describes how Demeter grieves for her daughter Persephone (also called Kore – 'maiden') who was first abducted by Hades and taken to the underworld, and then given to him in marriage by Zeus. The stricken mother deserts Olympus, the sphere of the gods, for the world of mortals, and goes to Eleusis where she asks the people to build a temple for her. Unappeased, Demeter brings devastation to crops and cattle, ignoring the intercessory pleas from Zeus' divine envoys. She asks only for a glimpse of her daughter. Zeus has no choice but to agree to Demeter's terms, and he sends his messenger Hermes to the underworld to negotiate with Hades. Hades agrees to allow Persephone to see Demeter, after ensuring first that by eating a pomegranate seed her return is guaranteed. Persephone pours out her heart to her mother and is consoled. Zeus decides to let mother and daughter remain together for two-thirds of each year, but Persephone must return to Hades for the remainder of the year. Content, Demeter allows the earth to be fertile once more, and the people of Eleusis continue their worship of her.

The importance of the Demeter and Persephone myth to Greek religion has been thought to stem from its connections with the seasons and the crucial issue of fertility. The centrality of female characters reflects the obvious links between women and birth. In her discussion of the contemporary interpretations of this myth, however, informed by feminist critique, Ross Kraemer notes how recent studies focus instead on the psychological issues raised in the *Hymn to Demeter*,[134] and see it as a reflection of women's actual lives.[135] She observes that, 'Regardless of the specific psychological dynamics of ancient Greek women, particularly free women, there can be no doubt that the myth expresses real tensions in the lives of Greek mothers and daughters.'[136] She points out that the depiction of marriage as beginning with rape is a common feature of Greek myth, as is the traumatic separation of young daughters from their mothers. The fathers are usually the instigators of this painful process, and although the anguish is well documented, marriage itself as the normative institution within society is not questioned.

The actual content of the Eleusinian mysteries remains hidden from the scrutiny of modern scholars, but there is evidence for many religious activities and devotions that focused on Demeter, many of which continued in popularity down into the Roman Empire.[137] The function of the Demeter myth would seem to be one of reinforcing traditional Greek practices regarding women's lives, in particular their rite of passage from daughter to wife, that is, from being a possession of a father to that of a husband.[138] A fragment from the early fifth century BCE that records Sophocles' words for a young woman, Procne, is just such a situation:

> When we are young in our father's house, I think we live the sweetest life of all humankind; for ignorance always brings up children delightfully. But when we have reached maturity and can understand, we are thrust out and sold away from the gods of our fathers and our parents, some to foreigners, some to barbarians, some to joyless houses, some full of reproach. And finally, once a single night has united us, we have to praise our lot and pretend that all is well.[139]

This extract resignedly depicts the Athenian woman's fate, and shows how the Demeter myth does seem to mirror this situation. Women are represented as being without direct power in this process, only able to intervene on the periphery. This can be illustrated by Demeter's failure to achieve more than a concession for her daughter to spend part of the year with her, rather than the full restoration of the relationship they had enjoyed before her abduction. The myth is a commentary on the way life is in Greek society, and by remembering it in the religious rites and devotions associated with it, the values of that society are reinforced. The popularity of the figures of Demeter and Persephone amongst women is a sign of their acquiescence with the *status quo*, and their survival into the time of the Roman Empire suggests that Greek values were still being used to support traditional values at a time even when they were being seriously questioned and challenged.[140]

As we saw from the last chapter Greek society did not provide women with a public role. Their sphere was the home where for most of the time they lived in segregation from male company. Unlike the women of Roman society, they could not be in the company of their husbands when they visited friends' houses, places of entertainment or the marketplace. Religious devotion was thus their only appearance in the public sphere, and because of this it was probably a particularly significant factor in their lives. Kraemer notes how rigorous Greek religion, particularly the devotions most associated with women, was in reinforcing gender roles, social positions and age categories. While the Demeter and Persephone devotions served the needs of women progressing from girlhood to womanhood, the devotions to Artemis and Hera focused on protection and success in childbirth, and were prohibited to slaves and foreigners. The third age of womanhood could have been represented by the goddess Hecate, regarded in negative terms as a hagged crone-like demon, and in positive terms as a goddess who could protect, grant success and act as an advocate. This leads Kraemer to comment: 'In the triad of Kore/Persephone, Demeter and Hecate, goddesses themselves reflect the trifold categorization of women as prefertile (the virgin), fertile (the mother), and postfertile (the crone).'[141]

The popularity of the Demeter and Persephone myth, and the religious devotions associated with them as goddesses, testified both to the close bonds between women in Greek society and to how society sacrificed those bonds to the 'higher' cause of marriages arranged by men. The participation of women in the 'male' cults of Adonis and Dionysus suggests a certain dissatisfaction among women with their given status and role. Kraemer argues that, 'The worship of these male deities appears to provide women some opportunities to relax the specific constraints of insulation and increase autonomy.'[142] Neither Adonis nor Dionysus belongs to the essentially Greek hierarchy of gods, the Olympians; both have foreign pedigrees. Adonis has a semitic name and is regularly associated with the dying and rising deities of the ancient Near East.

As we have noted, religious observance was the only public activity where women could participate in Greek society, in some cases alongside men. In the male deity cults, gods were closely associated with goddesses, Adonis with Aphrodite his consort, Dionysus with Semele his mother. Some of these cults had ceremonies designed to encourage women to be uninhibited. Dionysus, for instance, was the god of wine and his worship naturally provided occasions for such behaviour, as this verse describing his female worshippers attempting to convert the city of Thebes shows:

> O Thebes, nurse of Semele,
> wreathe yourselves with ivy!
> Abound in bryony, green and brilliant with berries!
> Make yourself a bacchant with branches
> of oak and pine and
> fringe your dappled fawn skins with tufts of white wool!
> Treat your violent wands with reverence.
> The whole earth will dance at once!
> Bromius is he who leads his bands to the mountains
> where the crowd of women waits
> driven from their looms and shuttles
> by Dionysus!
>
> Euripides, *Bacchae* 105–19[143]

Rituals associated with Dionysus range from the rather sedate *Lenaia* (from *lenai*, another name for Dionysus' devotee *maenad*), where food and drink offerings accompany the ceremonial entry of the god's mask into the sanctuary for worship, to the more erotic *Anthesteria*, the winter wedding festival between Basilinna, the wife of the Archon Basilius, and Dionysus.

More extreme, however, were the rites associated with Dionysus that are recorded in the *Bacchae*, a play written as early as the late fifth century BCE, by Euripides. The 'bacchae' are the women followers of Dionysus, and they are also known by the more pejorative term 'maenads', from the verb *mainomai*, 'to be driven mad'. The myth of Dionysus is recounted in many ancient sources,[144] but the classic description of Dionysiac ecstasy was drawn by Euripides whose work was the source for accounts in later centuries.

According to Euripides' *Bacchae*, Dionysus introduced his rites in Thebes in order to avenge the injustices perpetrated against his mother Semele who had been dishonoured by the lies spread about by her sisters, Agave, Autonoe and Ino. On hearing that Semele was pregnant, the sisters discounted her own truthful account that she had conceived through Zeus, and instead told the story that she had been impregnated by a mortal. They said that her father, Cadmus, had persuaded her to lie and say it was Zeus. This, the sisters explained, was why Semele had been struck dead by one of Zeus' thunderbolts. However, Dionysus explains that his mother had, in fact, been the victim of the jealous Hera's thunderbolt. This was shot while his father Zeus grabbed him from his mother's womb, saving him from being a victim of Hera's jealous plot.

The revenge of Dionysus for his mother's honour is directed at his aunts. He induces insanity on them, and they and bands of women followers dance off to the countryside, wearing fawnskins with snakes around their necks, leaves and branches in their hair and each with a wand (*thyrsus*) in their hand. They feed wild animals with their breast milk before they behave wildly: ripping animals apart, wrecking villages, abducting children. They are impervious to the missiles hurled at them by the men of the villages who suffer terrible wounds from the women's wands. There are many such details recounting the anarchic behaviour of the bacchae as they maniacally devour the countryside.

Dionysus' revenge reaches its climax when his aunt Agave dismembers what she perceives to be a wild animal, but is actually her own son Pentheus in disguise. She is allowed to regain her sanity in time to recognize the torn body of her son just as she brings it to her father. The outcome is that the dynasty of Cadmus is destroyed, Agave exiled, and the city of Thebes becomes a centre for the worship of Dionysus.

The account of Euripides implicitly details many of the features associated with Dionysiac rites known to us from artistic impressions on vases down the centuries,[145] the lively dancing and dressing up in animal skins and various types of vegetation. The actual ceremonies remained the secret knowledge of initiates, and this secrecy motif was intensified by the rites being practised at night, attracting many rumours and exaggerated imaginings from those outside the cult. The sexual nature of these rites would seem to belong to the fantasies of external perception rather than the reality of the religion itself.

Classical scholars have had to weigh the evidence of the written accounts of the Dionysiac myths against what has been discovered from classical representations in various art works. There is insufficient external evidence from Euripides' time to determine whether he was basing his account of the myth on the actual practices of the Dionysus cult as he knew it. It may be that his work actually provided the descriptions on which later rites were based. According to the myth, women are the main participants, the bacchae. Pentheus is the only man mentioned, but he appears not as a man, but disguised as a wild beast. There is some evidence for male participation, namely, a late fifth/early fourth-century tablet found in southern Italy on a woman's grave mentions *bacchoi*, i.e. male bacchae.[146] But Kraemer calls for caution in applying a particular example of one individual's ritual for the afterlife as a general rule for the Dionysian cult.[147] She finds the fourth-century BCE evidence we have for the cult of Dionysus to be inconclusive on the question of gender participation, but reckons that evidence from Greek cities in Asia Minor in the third century for rites performed only by women is indisputable.

The evidence increases as we move into the Hellenistic period. Plutarch refers to women's ecstatic rites associated with Dionysus, describing how some women got trapped in severe weather while they were celebrating winter rites for Dionysus; and how a group of maenads had got carried away in their ecstatic state and had strayed into the territory of the enemy, but thanks to the protection of the women of that town, Amphissa, they survived.[148] It is also at this time that the cult of Dionysus spreads to Italy and then to Rome, noted later, in negative terms, by Livy.[149] It is Livy's account of one particular episode that gave bacchae-type rites their debauched, orgiastic and corrupt reputation. Livy wrote his account some hundred and fifty years after the events he describes, and is heavily dependent on the work of earlier Roman historians, characters such as the elder Cato,[150] whose reactionary comments on Roman life have already been discussed.[151] Balsdon, writing of the influences on Livy, makes the following observation:

> Among the historians who wrote towards the middle of the second century BCE and whose work has perished, was that self-confident and boorish embodiment of austere moral rectitude,

the elder Cato. It was his view, and the view of other Roman historians too, that they lived in a period of increasing moral decline. Opinions differed only as to the moment at which the rot set in.[152]

Livy's later reconstruction of 'the bacchanalian scandal' betrays many traces of the moral outrage of his historian forefathers. The events took place in 186 BCE and concerned a young man named Publius Aebutius whose father and guardians had died and whose inheritance had been mishandled by his stepfather and mother.[153] In order to prevent Aebutius from taking action against them, they decided to find a way of keeping him in their control. Their solution was to initiate him into the bacchanalia. Aebutius' mother, Duronia, explained to her son that when he had been ill she had made a vow, promising that she would initiate him into the bacchic ritual if he recovered.

Now Aebutius had a mistress, a former slave girl, Hispala Fecenia, who had been supporting him since his fortune had been plundered. Aebutius explained to Hispala about his mother's vow and that, due to this religious obligation, she would not be seeing him for a while. When Hispala discovered what rite it was to be she was horrified because, as a slave girl, she had been initiated into it when she accompanied her mistress to the sanctuary.

Aebutius returns home and in the presence of his mother and stepfather refuses to undergo initiation. They react by evicting him from the house, and he flees to his aunt Aebutia where he confides in the consul Postumius. Eventually Hispala is questioned also and the story develops into a full-scale inquiry into the bacchanalian rituals that took place after dark in the grove of Semele. Hispala's extreme reluctance to cooperate in the investigation reflects her fear of the consequences of betraying the secrets of the bacchae. Not only would the gods seek vengeance, but the worshippers might tear her limb from limb. She only speaks after being promised that she will be able to live safely in exile from Italy.

Her testimony describes how the shrine to Semele had originally been a women's shrine to which men were not admitted. There were three festivals a year where bacchanalian rites were celebrated at daytime and where married women were priestesses. Then a priestess from Campania, Paculla Annia, as a result of a divine revelation, initiated men for the first time, and the three ritual practices a year became five a month and were celebrated at night. Male and female celebrating side by side at night encouraged crime and debauchery of an unnatural type, according to Livy's account. Any reluctance to participate resulted in death. Initiates had to be under the age of 20, a rule presumably designed to gain the most impressionable members of society. The rites were characterized by frenzied behaviour by both sexes, and the women wore their hair loose and wild in contrast to the controlled coiffure of dignified Roman women.[154] After giving her evidence, Hispala was persuaded to reside in safety in the house of the consul's mother-in-law. Livy comments that as a result of Hispala's testimony the rites of the bacchae were outlawed, and many initiates imprisoned or executed.

Livy's account, however, must be set alongside the evidence of a decree of Senate. The Senate decree, for example, allows for leniency in the case of many individuals,[155] while Livy's account is highly emotive and would seem to bear the stamp of a type of xenophobia that developed as a reaction to Greek infiltration of Roman culture. The cult of Cybele, the Great Mother goddess, which was also unpopular in the same quarters as being Greek in origin, although not as anarchic as Livy's descriptions of the Dionysian bacchae, did include the practice of male self-castration and gross ornamentation for its male priests. The rites associated with Cybele are particularly significant in the context of gender construction, and will be discussed in a later chapter.[156]

Isis was the focus of another oriental cult imported into Roman culture. It had particular associations for women, in terms both of its priesthood and its popularity. The Egyptian myth that lies at the heart of the rites of Isis is a familiar one of sibling rivalry.[157] According to Plutarch's version, a king of Egypt, Osiris, had a brother, Typhon, and two sisters, Isis and Nephthys. Typhon conspires against his brother to gain power, luring him into an ornate treasure chest which he then seals and throws into the Nile. Isis, who had been incestuously involved with Osiris since they shared the same womb, goes looking for her lost brother. In her search she discovers that Osiris had also been on sexual terms with their sister Nephthys who had given birth to a son. She had left this baby exposed to die because she was actually married to her other brother, the villain Typhon. Isis saves the child, named Anubis, who remains with her and becomes her attendant and protector. Continuing her search for Osiris, Isis finds the treasure chest on the river shore at Byblos, and she becomes pregnant, presumably by her dead brother, or she may have already been pregnant by him; Plutarch does not clarify this detail. Their child is Horus, a very popular and significant figure in the rites associated with Isis and Osiris. Meanwhile Typhon comes across the treasure chest again, opens it and cuts up his brother's body into fourteen pieces which he scatters over the waters of the Nile. Distraught with news of this act, Isis combs the river marshes for the pieces, and finds them all save for the penis which some fish had eaten. Osiris then returns from the underworld and trains his son Horus to avenge Typhon on his behalf.

During the Hellenistic period, the Greeks identified Isis with Aphrodite, although she was much more than the goddess of love. 'The single goddess Isis embodied forces and exercised powers that the Greeks had distributed among many deities, both male and female.'[158] Transported to Rome, the Isis and Osiris rites understandably lost their connections with the Nile which had been significant, according to Plutarch, in the Egyptian cult. One dramatic rite in which the image of the river setting survived, however, was the March festival of *Navigium Isidis*, richly described by Apuleius towards the end of the second century CE.[159] A great procession of women and men, mostly dressed in white linen, followed by priests carrying the sacred objects and the gods themselves (a person dressed as Anubis and a cow representing Isis), made their way to a nearby river side; in Apuleius' account it was at the port of Cenchreae. A grand sailing boat was then purified by the high priest, and launched by the devotees. Other rites, for example the festival of *Isia*, retained the clear pattern of the myth, re-enacting the death of Osiris and the mourning and searching of Isis, culminating in the joy of resurrection. In addition to the festivals there were daily rituals at the temple where the figure of Isis was cleaned and dressed.

The Isis cult is not one that was exclusive to women, but, because two of the central characters, Isis and Nephthys, were female, women were given prominence in any ceremony that re-enacted the myth. Apuleius' description makes it clear that the cult of Isis was popular amongst women of all classes in Italy and the western provinces: 'then followed a great crowd of the Goddess' initiates, men and women of all classes and every age, their pure white linen clothes shining brightly' (Apuleius 18). Pictorial evidence also exists; for example, in a first-century CE wall painting from Pompeii a ritual at a temple of Isis is depicted and the popularity of this cult among women is reflected by the number of female figures represented.[160]

The central focus of the cult of Isis is the relationship between a man and a woman. Its incestuous nature serves to intensify the bond.

It embodies perfect heterosexual love that triumphs even over death, and, as such, it supports the Greco-Roman ideal of the foundation of the family. It is tempting to interpret civic support of this cult as an attempt to endorse the family and the *status quo* of society, and women's devotion to it as their acquiescence. Kraemer discusses various contemporary explanations for the particular appeal the Isis cult held for women. Perhaps a new focus on the nuclear family was the result of the disintegration of Hellenistic city states. Alternatively, the cult so perfectly represented the expectations of Greco-Roman women that it provided sanction and sanctification for their lives,[161] or maybe, as a marginalized oriental cult, its devotion was attractive to women who felt marginalized themselves. I would suggest another factor might have been that as a result of the countless military campaigns that characterized the years of the late Republic and early Empire, for so many women married life meant in effect widowhood. Living in that reality, rites which focused upon a couple that are separated by death yet reunited by a love stronger than death would surely have special significance for women.

In the context of women's participation in religion in the Greco-Roman world special mention has to be made of the virgins dedicated to the goddess Vesta. Vestal Virgins have furnished popular images and language down the centuries of western culture, and this familiarity has tended to give them a prominence out of keeping with the religious situation of their time. Their numbers, for example, were minimal: 'To invent a parallel, you would have to imagine that in the whole of modern Italy there was only one body of nuns, and that there were a mere six members of that body.'[162] They were a crucial factor, however, in Roman perceptions of the relationship between their city and the deities who protected it. The Vestal Virgins were chosen for their unique office before they had reached puberty, between the ages of 6 and 10. Once chosen they were celibate for thirty years, and devoted to the task of tending the sacred fire of the round temple of Vesta at the centre of the Forum. This shrine was the oldest of the Forum, and according to the account of Pliny the Elder, noting, however, that as a man he would have had no access to the shrine, it had no image of the goddess Vesta but contained a sacred phallus (*fascinum*), the *Di Magni*, that is, household gods of Troy, and a sacred Trojan image of Athena known as the Palladian.

The Vestal Virgins as a group are unique in social, political and religious terms. Mary Beard, in recognizing their distinctive status, has noted similarities between them and aristocratic males, as well as affinities with unmarried women and matrons. These are reflected by their dress, their legal status and the rituals they perform.[163] Plutarch's description depicts their exceptional position as women:

> They had power to make a will in the lifetime of their father; they had a free administration of their own affairs without guardian or tutor ... when they go abroad they have the *fasces* [a bundle of rods and an axe used in capital punishment, and symbolizing the power to carry out that punishment] carried before them; and if in their walks they chance to meet a criminal on his way to execution, it saves his life, upon oath made that the meeting was an accidental one, and not concerted or of set purpose. Any one who presses on the chair on which they are carried is put to death.[164]

The celibacy of the Vestal Virgins was jealously guarded, and Plutarch goes on to describe how, if any of their number was discovered to have broken her vow, she was ceremonially buried alive:

> A narrow room is constructed underground to which a descent is made by stairs; here they prepare a bed and light a lamp and leave a small quantity of food, such as bread, a pail of milk, and some oil; so that a body which has been consecrated and devoted to the most sacred service of religion might not be said to perish by such a death as famine.

Then Plutarch describes how the victim is placed on a litter and tied down with cords to limit her struggle and cries as she is taken to the Forum:

> When they come to the place of execution, the officer looses the cords and then the high priest lifting his hands to heaven, pronounces certain prayers to himself before the act and then he brings out the prisoner, being still covered, and placing her upon the steps that lead down to the cell turns away his face with the rest of the priests. The stairs are drawn up after she has gone down, and a quantity of earth is heaped up over the entrance to the cell, so as to prevent it being distinguished from the rest of the mound. That is the punishment of those who break their vow of virginity.

As can be seen from this, the high priest of the cult was male. In fact, the first Emperor, Augustus, was elected high priest in 12 BCE, and when this happened he created a shrine to the goddess Vesta in his own home on the Palatine. As we noted above, even the Emperor as high priest of the cult could not enter the shrine: that privilege was reserved for its female virginal attendants. He could as high priest, however, carry out their execution. This office could be seen as yet another element in Augustus' search for infinite power and immortality.

The power of the Vestal Virgins was a visible reality in many aspects of the lives of these females, but these were, in effect, young women without any sexual autonomy. They were offered in the selection process for the Vestal Virgins at the age of 6 by their parents, and, if chosen, they were committed to that life for a minimum of thirty years. As we have seen, their sexuality was controlled, or rather restricted, by the state, and any independent act to exercise their own will in this respect was met with execution by the hand of the male high priest. They did receive abundant privileges, attending senatorial dinner parties, going to the theatre with the imperial women, guarding precious documents of state. These privileges reflect the belief among Romans that these women were the true guardians of Rome: its purity and its potency. 'Certainly the Vestals sacrificed their own years of fertility to transfer their powers to Rome and the renewal of the generations.'[165]

The order of the Vestals was the only order of cult officials which was full time in Greco-Roman religion, and for these women full time meant their whole time.[166] A comment made by Mary Beard throws light on the 'full-time' nature of their religious office, and offers an explanation that comes somewhere near accounting for their unique commitment. She understands them as symbols and realities of ambiguity, manifested in their central role in maintaining the constant fire of Vesta within the mysterious shrine. She regards their transformation from young girls to Vestal Virgins as a type of transsexual process, comparable to the status and function of castrated men of the Magna Mater cult: 'men who were not "men" standing next to women who were not "women"'.[167] The Vestals' ambiguous sexual status in legal terms reflected their mediation between opposites: heaven and earth, purity and impurity, life and death, male and female. Their 'crossing over' from female nature to male culture symbolically fuses and engages all fragmented power for generating the dynamic and ever-expanding Roman Empire.

Another popular cult in Rome, associated with Roman matrons, was the cult of Bona Dea, the 'good goddess'. Her proper name was Fauna, understood as the daughter, or sometimes the wife of Faunus, otherwise known as Pan. She was worshipped exclusively by women, and her official yearly nocturnal rite was celebrated in early December in the house of the chief magistrate, led by his wife and assisted by the Vestals. This was a cult particularly associated with the *matronae* who were distinguished as a group by their 'respectability', that is, they were legally married and therefore able to produce rightful heirs, and they were freeborn.[168] They wore particular clothes: long dress (*stola*) and a distinctive headband.[169] They were involved in many religious festivals in Rome but the Bona Dea cult was a particular focus for them. In fact the Bona Dea cult would seem to have been elitist not only in terms of gender but also in terms of its popularity among the freed classes. Our knowledge of the Bona Dea cult is, as so often, restricted to male descriptions of which we have to be wary since men were excluded from all the preparations and celebrations. One detailed account comes from Cicero who was directly involved since his residence, as magistrate, was the venue for the December rite. His account is highly subjective because at the time, 63 BCE, he was involved in a political struggle and he interprets particular happenings as signs to himself from the goddess.[170] The next year a man tried to infiltrate the festival, this time at the house of Julius Caesar who held the praetorship that year, by disguising himself as a female harp player. The infiltrator was recognized as Clodius, a prominent member of Roman elite society, whose aim, it was alleged, was to seduce Caesar's wife during the celebrations. He denied the charge and was found not guilty, a result, according to Cicero, that came from a bribed jury.

This event formed the basis of Juvenal's lively and erotic pastiche,[171] which may be seen as a lurid undermining by male commentators of female religious practices. It would seem to be the case, however, that these rites did allow women an opportunity to behave in a more free and unrestrained manner than public events would normally allow. Brouwer paints a convincing picture from all our available evidence of the December rites, at which women could drink undiluted wine, for example, and have boisterous 'sing-songs' accompanied by female musicians. This party atmosphere developed when the ritual part of the evening, the sacrifice of a pregnant pig in front of the cult statue of Bona Dea brought from the temple, was completed.

In describing the nature of Greco-Roman religious practices we are confronted with diversity and variety on an imperial scale. Our period of study is one of expansion both in the late Republic and the early Empire, and this expansion meant the discovery for Roman society of myths, cults and rituals, from every corner of the known and conquerable world. Even prior to that time, Hellenism had been absorbed and had exported along with its colonies an exotic variety of religions.

It is impossible to make general observations about religious practices at this time in the light of their extreme diversity, added to which we have such a number of variables such as local political interest, geographical features, fusion of residual culture with imported practices. Our main interest in this section has concerned women's involvement in Greco-Roman religion, which we have broadened with a glance at legend and poetry that reflected life and belief for women in antiquity. We have found religions that expressed women's experience, emotional and physical, from becoming young women, to their lives as mature matrons. We have found that religion is not only a reflection of those experiences but a prescriber and reinforcer of them.

5

THE RELIGION OF
JEWISH WOMEN

Jerusalem is consciously presented by Judaism as the centre of its faith: it is the capital of God's chosen land; where God's chosen king should live, and, most importantly, where God's holiness dwells in a unique manner. The latter refers to the inner sanctuary of the temple, the Holy of Holies which is only entered by one person, the high priest, once a year on the Day of Atonement.

In our earlier discussion of women in Jewish society, any function for them in cultic terms would seem to be out of the question, particularly when we bear in mind both the taboo about menstruation, and the emphasis on the ritual purity of the priests.[172] The concept of priesthood in Judaism was restricted by virtue of its being an inherited function. There were two 'priesthoods': Levite and Zadokite. The former was divided into two categories: the Levites whose function was one of servicing the cult, including cleaning up the sanctuary and the precincts, and then the Levites who were descended from Aaron, Moses' brother, who carried out the regular and daily sacrifices. The priesthood of Zadok, installed in Jerusalem by King David, traditionally provided the cult with its high priest.

When we look at reconstructions of the second temple in Jerusalem, which existed from 515 BCE to 70 CE, we can observe a clearly defined system of segregation between high priest, Levites, Jewish men, Jewish women and Gentiles. Within the temple precincts there existed a Court of Gentiles, a Court of Women, a Court of Israelites, a Court of Priests and finally the Holy of Holies where only the high priest could enter.[173] The Court of Women did not segregate men from women since men had to pass through this section to enter the Court of Israelites. The effect of having a women's section was to clearly separate women from the sacrificial activities. The Court of Gentiles was on the perimeter of the temple, separated from the area reserved for Jews by a balustrade a metre and a half high with gates and notices warning that Gentiles were forbidden to go beyond it on pain of death. One of these notices is still in existence: 'No foreigner is to enter within the forecourt and the balustrade around the sanctuary. Whoever is caught will have himself to blame for his subsequent death.'[174]

We can visualize the route, with its limits, taken by Jewish women worshippers through the various sections of the temple from this extract of Sanders' description of the temple precincts:

> They passed the balustrade and its warning notices, went up a flight of fourteen steps, crossed a terrace ten cubits deep, went up another five steps and came to the inner wall with its ten gates. Inside the inner wall lay, first, the Court of Women, 'open for worship to all Jewish women alike, whether natives of the country or visitors from abroad' (Josephus, *War*, 5.119). This was itself enclosed, and access for women was either from the north or the south: they could not use the central gate. The women's court was, according to the Mishnah, provided with a gallery, so that they could see over the heads of the men into the Court of the Priests (Middot 2.5).[175]

It would seem then, that Judaism, unlike the majority of the cults of the Greco-Roman world, excluded women not only from being active in the rituals of sacrifice and duties relating to the cult, but actually segregated them from the men observing the ritual, and the male priests performing it.

One piece of evidence that might call into question this androcentric picture of the Jewish cult is an inscription from Tell el-Yahudiyyeh in Egypt, that is, the ancient city of Leontopolis. In the light of beliefs held concerning the unique status of Jerusalem as *the* site for cultic Judaism, it is quite a surprise to discover that other temples existed in the Diaspora. Leontopolis is the best documented.[176] The inscription from Leontopolis is included in Bernadette Brooten's seminal work on this type of archaeological evidence. On the inscription, dated 7 June 28 BCE, is written, 'Marin, priestess [hierissa]'.[177] It could be that the Greco-Roman environment, particularly that of Egypt, the home of the Isis cult, did influence Jewish practice to the extent of allowing women of priestly families to function as priests. Brooten tentatively suggests that this could have been the case:

Could it be that the Jews of Leontopolis, living in a country in which there were women priests, had come, over the course of time, to accept as natural the cultic participation of Jewish women who claimed to be descendants of Aaron?[178]

Brooten's work is distinctive because she includes this type of interpretation and reconstruction where her predecessors had understood the same evidence in less challenging ways.[179] Evidence as tantalizing as the Leontopolis inscription is extremely rare, and far too sparse to allow us to conclude with confidence that women had any significant cultic function within Judaism. Rather firmer ground appears when we look at the synagogue movement that was rapidly gaining in popularity alongside the cult during our period.

Synagogues were the focal points for Jewish communities throughout Judea, Galilee and the Diaspora. Many would exist in a city that had a significant Jewish population. They were open and popular meeting places which fitted in well with the religious discourse and curiosity of the Greco-Roman world. Although Judaism by this time had suffered one serious religious pogrom as a result of Antiochus IV's enforcement of Hellenization in the middle of the second century BCE, and had faced hostility from the ignorance of its neighbours in the Diaspora, the relentless series of persecutions and holocausts that were to be its destiny down the centuries had not yet deeply scarred its relationship with the outside world. At this stage Judaism was openly confident among its neighbouring religions, and not averse to actively attracting new Gentile-born believers into its midst.

Such was the open nature of Judaism during our period that many Gentiles attached themselves to Jewish communities as full converts, or proselytes.[180] Other groups known as 'God-fearers' were distinguishable on the fringes of the religion. Both were phenomena of the synagogue movement, particularly in the Diaspora. Of their existence we are sure, but as to their exact number or what exactly distinguished a proselyte from a God-fearer less is known, and evidence is scarce and scattered. The demands on a convert to the Jewish religion were comparatively extreme in the Greco-Roman context where people moved easily between religious cults and belief systems. The Roman historian Tacitus comments, 'Jewish proselytes learnt nothing so quickly as to despise the gods, to abjure their fatherland, and to regard parents, children and kindred as nothing.'[181]

Despite the attraction of Judaism to many Gentiles, or perhaps to some extent because of it, there is a consistent disdain for Jews and their practices running through references in contemporary commentators and historians. As we have noted Jewish writers of the time, Josephus and Philo, consciously engaged in dialogue that represented Judaism in as attractive a light as possible.[182] They stressed, as we mentioned, the monotheistic nature of Judaism, rather than what might have appeared to the eyes of outsiders as strange idiosyncrasies, arguing that this central feature could enrich the religious thought of the Empire. Josephus in *Contra Apionem* argued that the Jewish religion provided perfect training for the model citizen.

Thus there seems to be an incongruity: on the one hand, we know there were significant numbers of Jewish proselytes and God-fearers in the Greco-Roman world; on the other hand, according to Roman writers, there was suspicion and intolerance for Judaism. To account for this ambivalence we must set Judaism alongside the other 'oriental' cults, such as those of Isis and Mithras. These were becoming increasingly popular during the years of the early Empire, and yet they too attracted opposition from reactionary commentators who felt the purity of Roman religion and culture was being undermined through the importation of foreign beliefs and practices.[183] We must add too that a special position of privilege was held by those who were part of the Jewish religion which allowed them to be exempt from worshipping the civic cults.

Our major concern at this stage in our study lies with women's active participation in the religious practices of Judaism during the late Republic and early Empire. In our analysis of the 'foreign' cults of the Greco-Roman world we observed, with the exception of the male-orientated Mithraism, that they held significant attractions for women devotees.[184] We must go on to see whether this applies to Judaism, or discover whether their role is distinctive among women in the oriental religions of the Empire in being explicitly excluded, or if their position is more complex.

As we noted in an earlier chapter,[185] the impression given, particularly by the legislation of Leviticus and its later interpretations, is that Judaism inherited a patriarchal system from ancient Israelite society and religion, which was reinforced by Hellenization. This would appear to mean that women were excluded from public activities, and played no significant role in religious matters. A comment made by Pieter van der Horst, in his analysis of relationships between Hellenism, Judaism and Christianity, presents an alternative reading of the evidence:

> it is important to keep in mind that a multitude of prohibitions mostly implies that the forbidden things did indeed take place. To put it another way: when it was so explicitly and emphatically prohibited that women receive or give formal education, that women move in public outside their homes, that women speak with men, that women have leading positions etc., then that certainly implies that all these things did happen. Where there is smoke there is fire.[186]

At this point we need to raise the question of whether in most synagogue buildings a women's gallery existed.[187] If this were the case, as attested by rabbinic sources and many modern-day scholars, that women were segregated from men, and restricted to seating some distance away from the central activities of synagogue worship, reading and preaching, then, obviously, women's participation would be restricted to that of distant observers. When Brooten addressed this question, she suggested that since it had been presupposed that a women's gallery existed in each ancient synagogue, as they do in contemporary orthodox synagogues, then archaeologists looked for one and made sure they found one.[188]

The evidence and impetus for endeavouring to find women's sections in ancient synagogues is partially circumstantial, stemming from our knowledge of the existence of a women's section, or court, in the second temple in Jerusalem.[189] As we noted earlier, however, this section did not segregate women from men, the two sexes mingled freely as men passed through the Court of Women on their way to the Court of Israelites. The Mishnah contains an interesting reference that implies that segregation developed in temple worship, rather than being there at the time of the actual building of the temple:

> Beforetime [the Court of Women] was free of buildings, and [afterward] they surrounded it with a gallery, so that the women should behold from above and the men from below and that they should not mingle together.
>
> (m.Mid.2.5)

It is not clear, however, that this refers to a regular and total separation of men and women in the temple precincts.[190] Rather, reading this statement in its wider context, and taking into account comments on the same issue from other rabbinic sources, this would seem to be referring to one particular ceremony that occurred on the first evening of the Feast of Tabernacles, and which actually took place in the Women's Court. This all-night celebration known as Beth haShe'ubah, or 'water-drawing', was, according to the Mishnah, the most joyous time of the festival calendar: 'They have said: He that never has seen the joy of the Beth haShe'ubah has never in his life seen joy' (m.Suk.5.1). The great levity prompted by this celebration caused concern, it would seem, among the temple authorities. In order to try to curb excess high spirits, a wooden gallery was built to separate women from men for this specific occasion referred to in passing in m.Suk.5.2 as the erecting of 'a great amendment', and was commented on in more detail in the talmudic commentary to this Mishnah. The rabbis were perplexed by this 'amendment' to the temple building since the precise measurements and building regulations for the temple were God-given:[191]

> But how could it be so? Is it not written, 'All this [do I give you] in writing as the Lord has made me wise by his hand upon me'? (1 Chron. 28.19). Rav answered, 'They found a scriptural verse and expounded it: "And the Lord shall mourn, every family apart; and the family of the house of David apart, and their wives apart" (Zech. 12.12). Is it not, they said, an *a fortiori* argument? If in the future when they will be engaged in mourning and the evil inclination will have no power over them, the Torah nevertheless says, "men separately and women separately," how much more so now when they are engaged in rejoicing and the evil inclination has sway over them.'
>
> (b.Sukk.51b-52a)

The argument can be explained as follows: God commanded that in the context of mourning, a time when there is no apparent evil inclination, that is, no sexual arousal between the sexes, men and women should be apart. If this is God's will in the case of mourning, how much more would it be appropriate in the case of extreme revelry? Thus one particular annual exception when the sexes were formally separated is taken as normative practice for the temple, and in turn, as the prototype for synagogue practice.

In this context reference has been made to Philo of Alexandria's description of a monastic type of Judaism which practised celibacy in various parts of Egypt, notably in the outskirts of Alexandria. It had both male (Therapeutae) and female (Therapeutrides) members who had left the cities to follow a contemplative life. The balance between male and female monastics singles out this movement from the Essenes. The latter too promoted celibate, monastic life for one class of membership, but the instructions and lifestyle for that group were intended for men only.[192] In his description of the Therapeutae and Therapeutrides Philo mentions a weekly gathering where both groups are present, and he notes that they are separated by a barrier.[193] It would be unconvincing to use this to support the idea that there was a general principle widespread in Judaism for segregation of the sexes during synagogue worship. This group is highly unusual in a Jewish context both in promoting celibacy and the contemplative life, and Brooten points out that we have to take account of why Philo needed to describe it:

> The very tenor of Philo's description of this group of people suggests that he was telling his readers something they did not already know. Whether written for Jewish or non-Jewish readers, the report on this exotic sect is an introduction to customs not widely practiced.[194]

Thus it would seem that we are far from a position where we can presume that men and women were carefully and frequently segregated for worship in either the temple or the synagogue. In the case of the latter, we are now in a position to assess the possibility of women taking a full part in the organization and activities of the ancient synagogues.

The most significant work that has been done in respect of this question, and in regard to the period of Roman dominance in the ancient world, is that of Brooten.[195] Her thesis is based on evidence from nineteen Greek and Latin inscriptions that date from 27 BCE to possibly as late as the sixth century CE. In these inscriptions women are given the titles 'head of the synagogue', 'leader', 'elder', 'mother of the synagogue' and 'priestess'. This evidence was not discovered by Brooten. A number of the inscriptions had been known to scholars for some time, and she notes that, 'According to previous scholarly consensus, Jewish women did not assume positions of leadership in the ancient synagogue. Scholars have therefore interpreted the titles borne by women in these inscriptions as honorific.'[196] What Brooten offers is an alternative interpretation of this evidence.

In relation to the title 'head of the synagogue', she uses three inscriptions, one from Smyrna, Ionia (*circa* second century CE); another from Kastelli Kissamou, Crete (fourth to fifth century CE); and one from Myndos, Caria (fourth to fifth century CE). Three women heads of synagogues are mentioned respectively: Rufina, Sophia and Theopempte. In the case of Rufina the inscription reads:

> Rufina, a Jewess, head of the synagogue, built this tomb for her
> freed slaves and the slaves raised in her house. No one else has
> the right to bury any one [here]. If someone should dare to do,
> he or she will pay 1500 denars to the sacred treasury and 1000
> denars to the Jewish people. A copy of this inscription has been
> placed in the [public] archives.[197]

Brooten comments:

> This grave, the persons to be buried in it, the marble plaque
> with its official legalistic language, and the high fine to be
> imposed, all point to the wealth and influence of this woman.
> We know nothing about her marital status, but it is noteworthy
> that no husband is mentioned; she has drawn up the deed in
> her own name.[198]

Brooten does not doubt that Rufina held the office of the head of her synagogue, and that this office would have meant, according to sources from the Mishnah, and New Testament accounts of synagogue practice,[199] that she would have been learned in matters of Jewish law, she would have had particular responsibility for the spiritual direction of the community, she would have taught in the community, and she would have been involved in decisions relating to the building and restoration of synagogues. Brooten infers from this evidence that wealth was a factor in holding this office.

Brooten refers to earlier interpretations of the title which fall into three categories: (i) women received the title through their husband's status; (ii) in the later period such titles were honorific; (iii) in the case of women the title must be honorific. Brooten deals convincingly with all three explanations. For the first one she notes that no husband's name is mentioned alongside the women: they all appear independently of any spouse. For the second, she argues there is no evidence to support it, and comments rather cynically, 'One has the suspicion that the theory of the later development into an honorific title was created expressly for the purpose of interpreting the Rufina inscription and then came in quite handy for the Theopempte inscription when that was discovered some years later.'[200]

Having discussed the possibility that exceptional, usually wealthy, Jewish women in the Greco-Roman period fulfilled prominent roles in some synagogues, we must translate this knowledge into the context of the Jewish communities. In essence the synagogues were the communities. The synagogue building, the choice of elders, the type of worship and education available are all a reflection on the community it served. If it were possible in some contexts for women to hold key positions in relation to the synagogue then they would be key figures within the community, respected, from what we can glean from the inscriptional evidence, in the first instance, for their wealth and judgement.

The Jewish home could be considered the nucleus of the religion, with the synagogue, and even the cult, being extensions of it. Conversely, a Jewish community is, in essence, a network of Jewish families. Furthermore, many important cultic practices centre on occurrences in the home: the birth of a child, a sin against a relative, and so on. Since the home was primarily the domain of the women, the religious practices associated with it give prominence to women. Activities such as preparing the home for the annual Passover meal are a woman's responsibility, involving cleaning the home thoroughly to ensure no leaven exists in it so that the bread that is consumed at the meal is free from any even accidental action of the leaven. Each week the Sabbath is inaugurated by the matriarch lighting a lamp or candles, one of three actions whose omission, it was taught, could lead to the death of the woman in childbirth. The other two were for the woman to keep a strict account of her menstrual cycle, and for her to ensure that a portion of the unbaked dough be set aside as an offering. The Mishnah expresses this dire warning very concisely:

> For three transgressions do women die in childbirth: for heed-
> lessness of the laws of the menstruant, the Dough-offering, and
> the lighting of the [Sabbath] lamp.

> (m.Shab.2.6)

In a recent study on mishnaic teaching regarding women Judith Wegner asks why these three prescriptions should have such a fatal threat attached to them. She concludes that this is because they all have serious repercussions for a woman's husband:

> The three cultic duties listed here, like other biblical precepts,
> are primarily incumbent on *men*, but they happen to be *the
> three rites most often delegated to women*. . . . A *wife's* neglect
> of these religious duties makes her *husband* a transgressor.[201]

Wegner does note that these three duties are 'time-contingent precepts', that is commandments that are not binding on women.

Therefore, to ensure that they are kept, and, most importantly, that their husbands are not in breach of a commandment, the women are threatened with death in childbirth.

It would seem that the three religious duties readily ascribed to women in the home are not necessarily a reflection of their being particularly highly esteemed in Judaism. Rather they are merely instrumental in ensuring that the central characters of the religion, the men, are protected from transgression and impurity. A comment in the Talmud, ascribed to rabbis of the early third century CE, epitomizes this attitude:

> Rav said to Rabbi Hiyya: 'With what do women earn merit?
> By making their sons go to the House of Assembly to learn
> scripture, and their husbands to the House of Study to learn
> Mishnah, and waiting for their husbands until they return from
> the House of Study.'
>
> (b.Ber.17a)

Nevertheless, we should bear in mind that it was religious practices in the home, usually performed by the mother, that provided the earliest religious awareness for the children. The Bible itself bids children to hear the instruction of their fathers *and* mothers: 'Hear, my child, your father's instruction, and do not reject your mother's teaching' (Prov.1.8); likewise, one of the Ten Commandments enjoins offspring to honour both parents (Ex. 20.12). Whatever the motivation, women did bear responsibility in terms of Jewish religious practice in the home, and for most women this would be the full extent of their influence.

Brooten's work on the inscriptions, particularly those relating to the first two centuries CE, is extremely important when we are attempting to reconstruct Jewish structures and practices of the time, and, more precisely, women's roles within them, especially since evidence of Judaism during this period is so scarce. We have Jewish biblical texts which date, in the main, from the fifth to the second century BCE, that is before the period of Roman pre-eminence, and then we have rabbinic literature dating from 200 to 600 CE, with the Talmudim being edited at the end of that time-span. We have examples of Jewish writers from the first century CE: Philo of Alexandria and Josephus; but their work is apologetic in nature, designed for Roman consumption to attract respect and protection for the Jewish religion. They do not provide us with information that usefully and directly furnishes our knowledge of the practical and structural workings of the religion in relation to women's lives.

Also, we have the Dead Sea Scrolls from Qumran believed to be the product of an Essene community founded in the middle of the second century BCE by some who had left Jerusalem disillusioned by the political compromises made by the incumbent high priest and his family.[202] While we are not in a position to speak of a 'normative' Judaism until the ascendancy of rabbinic Judaism at the end of the first century CE, it is clear that the Essenes were a factional group with particular interests and beliefs that did not represent the majority of religious Jews at the time.

Likewise, we possess a body of literature from the middle to the end of the first century CE written by Jews from the Diaspora and possibly Judea and Galilee. These texts are found, however, in the Christian Bible and form the main ingredients of what is known as the New Testament. These Jews, while belonging under the broad umbrella of pluralistic Judaism as it existed until the destruction of the second temple in 70 CE, developed an identity that set their particular beliefs outside the parameters of Judaism, noting that those parameters shrank considerably as a result of the tragic outcome of the war with Rome. Even before 70 CE the followers of Jesus of Nazareth distinguished themselves from the majority of Jews, not so much by their practices as by their beliefs. These beliefs included the conviction that Jesus of Nazareth was the true Messiah, the anointed one of God, who, having been crucified and then raised from the dead, was to return to the earth from the right hand of God in heaven in full messianic glory and bring about the cataclysmic end of human history. The idea that God's chosen Messiah could have been put to death by crucifixion like a common criminal was an anathema to most Jews,[203] and this conviction of Jesus' followers, coupled with their non-alignment with the Jews of Palestine in their offensive against the Roman army in 66–70 CE, meant that this new religious phenomenon of the first century soon became a thorn in the flesh for the majority of Jews. The messianic claims and the belief that the end-time had actually arrived in embryonic form and would reach its apocalyptic climax in the very near future,[204] means that the texts this group produced are not indicative of much of Judaism, and only occasionally and unconsciously furnish us with useful material for creating a picture of Judaism in the first century CE. These texts are essentially evangelical in nature, written with an urgency to convince people of the truth of their claims about Jesus of Nazareth before the imminent final act of the eschaton.[205]

One Jewish biblical text that does appear to provide us with a clear example of female characters making an historical contribution to the Jewish religion is the *Book of Ruth*. This text focuses on female characters and does treat them heroically, but does not take them too far beyond the bounds of credibility. The book is part of a strand of Jewish literature that does suggest a willingness on the part of Jewish writers in the Persian and Hellenistic periods to develop female characters, and to produce heroines for their stories. This seems to occur particularly in the context of literature produced as part of the constant internal Jewish debate concerning 'foreign' marriages. Those in favour of allowing on occasion a marriage between a Jew and non-Jew offered literary illustrations to show how beneficial rather than destructive this could prove to be.[206] *Ruth* describes the adventures of two women, Ruth and Naomi. Naomi is a Jewish woman whose husband had moved his family from Bethlehem in Judea to the land of Moab in order to escape famine. Naomi's husband and two sons had all died. The sons had been married to two Moabite women, Orpah and Ruth, who, in such circumstances, would have normally returned to their families to negotiate a new marriage. Naomi tells the two women to do precisely this since they could not expect her to produce any more husbands for them, and she planned to return to Judea where she had heard the famine had been relieved. Reluctantly Orpah agrees, but Ruth clings to Naomi saying:

> Where you go, I will go; where you lodge, I will lodge; your people shall be my people, and your God my God. Where you die, I will die – there I will be buried. May the Lord do thus and so to me, and more as well, if even death parts me from you!
>
> (1.16–17)

The most striking feature of the story of Ruth and Naomi is the description of the close bond that exists between the two women.

On reaching Bethlehem Ruth immediately attempts to find favour with Naomi's rich relative Boaz in order that she might find security for herself and her mother-in-law, and ensure that they can remain together. Together the two women plot Ruth's seduction of the unwitting but willing Boaz. Boaz's attraction for Ruth is strong, and further strengthened by his admiration for her loyalty to his kinswoman Naomi. He tells Ruth of another kinsman who has a closer

connection to Naomi and who has the right to any land or possessions in Bethlehem that had belonged to Naomi's husband. Having
been besotted by Ruth, Boaz takes charge of her and Naomi's affairs
and explains to this other kinsman that if he wanted to claim Naomi's
land he would have to take responsibility also for the two women.
The man happily hands over his entitlement of land to Boaz who
becomes the guardian of the women. He marries Ruth and the couple
bear a son. This child is recognized as kin for Naomi and the women
of Bethlehem rejoice at Naomi's change in circumstances:

> Blessed be the Lord who has not left you this day without next-
> of-kin; and may his name [the child's] be renowned in Israel!
> He shall be to you a restorer of life and a nourisher of your old
> age; for your daughter-in-law who loves you, who is more to
> you than seven sons, has borne him.

(4.14–15)

The happy ending is complete when the narrator tells us, 'Then
Naomi took the child and laid him in her bosom, and became his
nurse. The women of the neighbourhood gave him a name, saying,
"A son has been born to Naomi"'(4.16–17). The story closes
informing us that this child, Obed, is the grandfather of King David.
Thus the intervention of a 'foreign' woman meant that God's plan
for the birth of the greatest king in the history of the Israelite nation
was intact.

Since the advent of contemporary feminist interpretation of the
Bible in the 1970s the story of Ruth and Naomi has received a lot of
attention.[207] It is perhaps unique in biblical literature in providing a
description of a relationship between two women that can be used
as a model today in the context of feminist notions of sisterhood.
Together these two women recognize their weakness and powerlessness in a patriarchal society, yet overcome their dire situation by
using the customs and standards of that society to their best
advantage. This story does not attempt to challenge patriarchy,
rather, like the legend of Demeter and Persephone,[208] it takes for
granted the limited nature of women's status and their lack of power
in society, but also gains the maximum leverage with that situation
that is possible.

The story of Ruth and Naomi adds an interesting literary dimension to our knowledge of women's status in Jewish society, as
well as their status in religious terms. These women are, as far as
the narrator is concerned, instruments of God. Their actions and

thoughts epitomize perfect faith in the god of Israel. Like the patriarch Abraham they set off on a journey, trusting in their deity to protect them. The uniqueness of Ruth and Naomi's story lies in the further empowerment which comes from the unbreakable bond that forges them together. We have to allow that such a relationship is upheld and confirmed by Judaism, and that this story reflects the complex and ambivalent attitudes that the religion expresses concerning women's lives.

A unique example of a named woman mentioned in rabbinic literature who did exert influence and have her teachings recorded in a context that was the preserve of rabbis was Beruria. She belonged to a generation of scholars who were active during the first part of the second century CE. She was the daughter of Rabbi Hananya ben Teradion who was a colleague of the famous Rabbi Akiba and who shared the same fate at the hands of the Romans following the unsuccessful Bar Kochba revolt in 135 CE. She was married to Rabbi Meir, a disciple of Rabbi Akiba, whose teachings laid the foundation for the legal decisions collected in the Mishnah. It has been argued by contemporary scholars that the explanation for Beruria's exceptional place in the rabbinic tradition lies in the tales of her errant brother:

> It is related of the son of Rabbi Hananya ben Teradion that he took to evil ways and robbers seized him and killed him. After three days his swollen body was found; they placed him in a coffin, set him on a bier, took him into the city and paid him a eulogy out of respect for his father and mother.
>
> (b.Sem.49b)

Without a son of integrity and learning, the mantle of the father's scholarship passed to Beruria.[209] While this may explain why she then is accounted alongside the rabbis, it does not explain why her position is unique.

Beruria's status was not one of equality among her male rabbinic associates; although described as engaging in scholarship, she does not become part of the chain of tradition or rabbinic line of authority, neither does she take a place in the Beth HaMidrash (house of study). Elizabeth Sarah makes the point in this context that:

> while the teachings of the Rabbis are usually presented in the rabbinic texts as part of a debate or an exchange between two or more scholars, Beruria's scholarly opinions are either

presented on their own, albeit in a context in which other opinions are also recorded, or as a dialogue with her husband Rabbi Meir.[210]

There is even an example of how the ascription of a saying of Beruria seems to have been erased from a rabbinic text. The Tosephta is an early collection of rabbinic sayings and teachings contemporary with the Mishnah (200 CE), and when it records Beruria's opinion, on the question of the treatment of an unclean door-bolt, the account concludes with a commendation of her words by a great figure of her father's generation, Rabbi Yehudah: 'When they put the words before Rabbi Yehudah, he said: "Beruria spoke well"' (t.Kelim Baba Metziah 1.6). When the same discussion appears in the Mishnah, Beruria's name is omitted, and her teaching attributed to Rabbi Yehoshua ben Hananiah (m.Kel.11.4), who was active in rabbinic circles over a century before Beruria's generation.

There is a well-known discussion between Beruria and her husband Rabbi Meir concerning the attitude one should have towards those who sin against you. Beruria argues for a characteristically rabbinic notion of searching for repentance from sinful action:

> There were some highwaymen in the neighbourhood who caused him a great deal of trouble. Rabbi Meir prayed that they should die. His wife Beruria said to him: 'How can such a prayer be right? Because it is written, "Let sin be consumed" (Ps.104.35)? Does it say "sinners"? It is written "sins"! Look at the end of the verse where it says, "And let the wicked be no more." If the sins cease, then there will be no more sinners! Pray that they will repent.' He did pray for them and they repented.
>
> (b.Ber.10a)

Beruria's teaching is effective, and Rabbi Meir heeds her teaching. Another example follows this in b.Ber.10a where Beruria employs the same method of interpretation: using the end of a verse of scripture to throw light on the first part. Anne Goldfeld has suggested that in her use of this method we have an important clue as to why Beruria's opinions have been preserved in rabbinic texts. The collators of the Talmud were living some century and a half after her and her generation of scholars, and her method of interpretation, was popular at that later time.[211]

Elizabeth Sarah's account of Beruria paints a picture of a lonely religious scholar who, because of her sex, is unable to study with her male colleagues in the Beth HaMidrash, and who can teach no pupils. The rabbinic tradition allows for that picture to be painted without censoring Beruria; in fact, on one occasion it allows for her to tease one of the great sages on the question of women not being vocal:

> Rabbi Yose the Galilean was once on a journey when he met Beruria. 'By what road,' he asked her, 'do we go to Lydda?' 'Foolish Galilean,' she replied, 'did not the sages say this: "Engage not in much talk with women". You should have asked: "By which to Lydda?"'
>
> (b.Eruv.53b)

Here Beruria is reminding Rabbi Yose of a comment among the 'sayings of the fathers' in the Mishnah: 'the Sages have said: He that talks much with womankind brings evil upon himself and neglects the study of the Law and at the last will inherit Gehenna' (m.Avoth1.5).

However, as Elizabeth Sarah points out, this is not the end of our story of Beruria. Many generations later, in medieval times, she attracted the attention of rabbinic scholars, but this time there is no respect for her learning or admiration for her opinion, instead there seems only explicit misogyny at work. The main culprit is the French scholar Rashi. He bases his defamation of Beruria on an enigmatic comment in the Talmud. It comes at the end of a passage in b.Avodah Zarah 18a–b where Rabbi Meir has been attempting to free Beruria's sister who was being held against her will in a brothel, and at the close of the story we are told that Rabbi Meir fled to Babylon: 'Some say it was because of that incident that he ran to Babylon. Others say it was because of the incident about Beruria.' Rashi, in his commentary on the passage, offers this explanation for 'the incident about Beruria':

> One time, to reveal what the Sages said in Kiddushin 70b: 'Women are of light understanding', he went and said to her, 'your life is your end, respect their words.' He commanded one of his pupils to test her, to speak of sin, and he urged her for many days until she complied. When the plot was revealed to her, she hanged herself, and so Rabbi Meir fled because of being put to shame.

According to Rashi, Beruria dies at her own hand and Rabbi Meir flees and lives a life in exile, and all for encouraging a woman to be involved in rabbinic scholarship.

One contemporary opinion is that Beruria is a totally fictitious character, and the traditions associated with her, like the accounts of the Amazons we noted in an earlier chapter,[212] exist simply to show how absurd would be the notion of a woman rabbinic scholar.[213] Even if this supposition were to be true, the fact that time was spent creating this character and her opinions perhaps reflects a real need to silence the unnamed women who would dare to cross the boundary and debate their deity's teachings.

In the different contexts for observing religious practice, in the home, the synagogue and the cultic environment, a rather more complex picture of women's participation in Judaism than is usually assumed emerges. One pattern we can begin to discern is one which reflects the wider picture of the meeting of Hellenistic and Roman constructs of gender. The picture of a secluded women's domestic environment is one common to Hellenistic society. Its manifestation is more probable in an urban rather than an agrarian context. Ancient Israelite society would have been less divisive between the sexes since as an agrarian society division of labour and the nature of that labour meant that home and work-place were one and the same. It is an urban environment that separates work and home and allows for gender separation on the lines of public and domestic. When Judaism encountered the Hellenistic cities it began to reflect this pattern of urbanization of lifestyle, as we saw, for example, in the passage from Sirach where the daughters of the house are shut away from public gaze.[214]

Biology and lifestyle are both essential ingredients to constructing gender and gender roles. In the lives of women their boundaries cross, and so, if women are confined to women's quarters and live most of their time with female companions then their biological menstrual cycle is determined by those of their fellow females. This lifestyle can explain to some extent how the concept of menstrual regulations could develop in a society. In such a context menstruation would be more obvious when the majority of women were following the same cycle. The religion that upholds this type of secluded and single-gendered life for women is to some extent constructing their gender in biological as well as social terms, determining their hormone release and suppression.

As we noted in our first chapter, in the more open Roman

environment women were more visible. It is possible where the influence on Judaism, regarding the urban environment, was more Roman than Hellenistic, to observe a different picture. Here women can be wealthy in their own right, use their wealth to support their synagogues, and take up powerful positions within them. Greek models seem to be the overriding influence on Jewish attitudes to women, however, which may be due, at least in part, to the more frequent periods of open hostility that existed between the Jews and Rome, e.g. the expulsion of the Jews from Rome in the first half of the first century CE, the war against Rome in Palestine in 66–70 CE, and the final revolt in 135 CE.

Exceptionally, other factors can interrupt this pattern. For example, when the issue of 'foreign' marriage is at the centre of religious and social debate at the time of nascent Hellenistic influence, then female characters can still rise out of their obscurity and be set centre stage, as was the case with the story of Ruth and Naomi. Beruria, whether a fact or a fiction, was favoured by rabbis, most likely because of the method of interpretation associated with her, beyond her own generation and her name survives in the literature despite later attempts to discredit her.

The contemporary scholar of early rabbinic Judaism Judith Wegner in her book, *Chattel or Person?*, can find no clear answer to the question addressed in her title, finding as she does that the rabbis vacillate between the two alternatives. She laments that after 70 CE, when Judaism was creating a new identity for itself out of the ashes of the devastation of the temple and the blow that had been dealt to Jewish pride and confidence, the rabbis did not produce a different type of Judaism: 'sitting in their Grove of Yavneh, they could have created a utopia that abolished gender-based distinctions, like Plato in his Grove of Academe or Paul in his vision of the Kingdom of Christ in Gal. 3.28' (pp. 180–1).

This reference to St Paul the Christian apostle leads us into our next section where we will test whether such a positive picture of gender relations in that new religious movement of the first century CE can stand much scrutiny.

6

FROM DIVERSITY TO CONFORMITY

We begin the story of women and Christianity with the Jesus movement, and, as is common in so many contexts, looking for clues to understanding women's experiences here is a difficult task. There are pitfalls to avoid:

> Jewish and Christian scholars are prone to reconstruct early Judaism and Christianity not only in terms of what has survived as 'normative' in their own respective traditions but also as two distinct and oppositional religious formations. Since 'rabbinic' Judaism and patriarchal Christianity were the histor- ical winners among the diverse inner-Jewish movements, such a reconstruction insinuates that only these represent pre-70 Judaism in general and the Jesus movement in particular.[215]

Therefore we are faced with the challenge of trying to wipe our preconceptions of Christianity from our minds, and to begin afresh with a tableau of first-century Roman-occupied Palestine. Here the Jewish people, representing a spectrum of religious commitment and practice, were occupied with their everyday existence, and there existed in the back of the minds of many, and in the forefront of more than a few, the idea of ridding themselves of the burden of Roman domination. This was the climate from which Jesus emerged. As we noted in a previous chapter,[216] he came into the public gaze with an imperative message to the Jews to repent in the light of the dawn of their god's reign.

By taking even a cursory glance at the biblical accounts of Jesus' ministry found in the four gospels, it is immediately apparent how crucial the support of established Jewish scripture was to the message and person of Jesus. The books of the prophets were particularly apposite with their frequent references, often apocalyptic in tone, to

God's coming judgement and reign. In addition to Jesus' distinctive message concerning God's kingdom, his ministry, according to the minds of the biblical witnesses, was characterized by the presence of the divine spirit. This supernatural force, an attribute of God, which had also characterized the ministries of the prophets of the eighth century BCE and before, had come to be regarded as absent from the present age, and would only reappear in power when God instigated the period of the end-time. That is to say, Jewish belief concerning the manifestation of the spirit had become an eschatological hope. One passage from Jewish scripture, from the book of the prophet Joel, which was used by the early Christians and applied to their own context (Acts 2.17–21), encapsulates this hope:

> I will pour out my spirit on all flesh; your sons and your daughters shall prophesy, your old men shall dream dreams, and your young men shall see visions. Even on the male and female slaves, in those days, I will pour out my spirit.
>
> 2.28–29 (in the Hebrew Bible, 3.1–2)

It was in terms such as these that the early Christians understood Jesus' possession of the spirit of God, and their own:

> While it would be wrong to suppose that there was a unified view of the Spirit's activity in contemporary Judaism, there is good evidence to suppose that many Jews thought of the Spirit's activity as part of the past of Israel. Thus the inspiration by the Spirit was confined to the era of the prophets and would only be operative again when new prophets arose, in the Messianic Age.[217]

According to Christian belief the spirit was bestowed upon Jesus by God at his baptism.[218] It was also the hallmark of all who followed him,[219] and it enabled them to have similar supernatural powers to his:

> To each is given the manifestation of the Spirit for the common good. To one is given through the Spirit the utterance of wisdom, and to another the utterance of knowledge according to the same Spirit, to another faith by the same Spirit, to another gifts of healing by the one Spirit, to another the working of miracles, to another prophecy, to another the discernment of spirits, to another various kinds of tongues, to another the interpretation of tongues.
>
> (1 Cor. 12.7–10)

This charismatic feature of the Jesus movement, in organizational terms, goes against any notion of hierarchical structure, since the discerning factor in the group is one that is divinely, not humanly inspired. It allowed, as is made clear in the Joel passage, for the full inclusion of women. Men and women were to be endowed by the spirit at the end-time, and from what we can glean from the sparse information we have of the Jesus movement, this was the experience of that group. Hierarchical structures were challenged:

> Jesus called them and said to them, 'You know that among the Gentiles those whom they recognize as their rulers lord it over them, and their great ones are tyrants over them. But it is not so among you; but whoever wishes to become great among you must be your servant, and whoever wishes to be first among you must be slave of all.'
>
> (Mk 10.42–44)[220]

The new community of equals replaces the patriarchal family:[221] 'Whoever does the will of God is my brother and sister and mother' (Mk 3.35). This teaching is a radical alternative to the traditional familial concepts of Judaism in the Hellenistic world where family relationships were governed by power, and decreed according to age, gender and blood ties:[222]

> The child/slave who occupies the lowest place within patriarchal structures becomes the primary paradigm for true discipleship. Such true discipleship is not measured on the father/master position but on that of child/slave. This can be seen in the paradoxical Jesus saying: 'Whoever does not receive the *basileia* [kingdom] of God like a child [slave] shall not enter it' (Mk 10.15). This saying is not an invitation to childlike innocence and naivete but a challenge to relinquish all claims of power and domination over others.[223]

By reading these gospel sayings in terms of an egalitarian community, previous attempts to categorize the Jesus movement are being questioned, such as Gerd Theissen's notion of a 'love patriarchy'.[224] Fiorenza is particularly keen to dispel this as an accurate assessment of the phenomenon. It was highly effective when used in ecclesiastical, confessional circles to justify a continuation of hierarchy, with benevolent overtones, within the churches, supposedly mirroring the relationship between Jesus and the deity. Although there is evidence that Jesus saw parent/child as a suitable metaphor for human relations with the divine, the evidence that this should be carried over into the community to become the central organizational model, however, is not convincing. The theme of child-like dependence on God's grace is a radical image that demands setting aside human structures and materialism, and this is clear when the context of Jesus' assertion is taken seriously:

> 'Truly I tell you, whoever does not receive the kingdom of God as a little child will never enter it.' And he took them up in his arms, laid his hands on them, and blessed them. And as he was setting out on a journey, a man ran up and knelt before him, and asked him, 'Good teacher, what must I do to inherit eternal life?' Jesus said to him, 'Why do you call me good? No one is good but God alone. You know the commandments: "You shall not murder; You shall not commit adultery; You shall not steal; You shall not bear false witness; You shall not defraud; Honor your father and mother."' He said to him, 'Teacher, I have kept all these since my youth.' Jesus, looking at him, loved him and said, 'You lack one thing; go sell what you own, and give the money to the poor, and you will have treasure in heaven; then come, follow me.' When he heard this, he was shocked and went away grieving, for he had many possessions.
>
> (Mk 10.15–22)

Here the radical nature of Jesus' plea to his followers to be child-like is spelt out: all that society holds as precious is deemed to be worth nothing; and what society holds as worthless, poverty and powerlessness, was to be the model for human existence. This theme of anti-materialism closely bound up with anti-hierarchy is a feature of Jesus' teaching throughout the gospel accounts, and would seem to be an authentic strand of the earliest Christian tradition.

Such sensitivity to the central features of Jesus' teaching is essential if we are to discover the status of women within earliest Christianity. If, as a radical renewal movement, this group did challenge hierarchical structure as a basis for community organization, this would have an obvious bearing on women's status. In an egalitarian community the practice of marginalizing any group would not be possible. In the gospels women are often presented as illustrations of this point. Luke has the angel addressing Jesus' potential mother, a young Galilean peasant girl, as 'favoured one, the Lord is with you!' (1.28);[225] in John's gospel a Samaritan woman is the first to witness to Jesus' messianic identity;[226] in Mark a Syro-Phoenician woman persuades Jesus to heal her daughter, and by doing so extends his mission beyond the interests of Israel;[227] and, finally, the women disciples' primary witness to the resurrection is firmly rooted in the gospel tradition.

As we noted in our contextualization of the Jesus movement, it was essentially a Jewish renewal movement, characterised by strong millenarianism.[228] Jesus'concept of God's kingdom seemed to include an element of realized inauguration: that is, it had already begun in embryonic form in his ministry, and could be experienced by those who followed him (Lk 11.20). The new, radical a-familial teaching, for example, means that an alternative lifestyle, in contrast to the *status quo*, was already available. The energy that sustained this brief and zealous ministry was at heart urgently eschatological. Time was running out, the end was near, the righteous could already taste the first fruits of the new age if they repented, believed and followed Jesus. This was the context for women's participation. It was not slotted into existing society; nor was it merely a challenge to existing society which offered a non-sexist, non-hierarchical option for future generations. On the contrary, there was no future in human terms, according to Jesus' perspective. The future lay entirely in God's hands. It was God's will that was about to rip apart human structures, judge the culprits, and then impose the divine plan on a renewed world.

The new inclusion enjoyed by the women who followed Jesus, the new option for the 'sisters in Christ', was not intended to be a long-term solution to the centuries of patriarchy and exclusion. Rather it was an interim arrangement to reflect the universalism of God's imminent action. In pragmatic terms, women would have been a valuable resource in the new community, a point which should not be overlooked in an assessment of the motivation and practice of female inclusion in the Jesus movement. For itinerent groups of preachers, which would seem to be the characteristic lifestyle of the group in its earliest manifestation, sympathetic doors would be opened to them to break their journeys and receive hospitality. It would be women who would open these doors, as, for example, in the case of Mary and Martha in the gospels.[229] Such 'staging-posts' themselves became the initial foundation stones of the movement, providing places for communication and meeting. The tradition of households forming the nucleus in villages and towns for Christian communities was passed down to the urban environment, and this phenomenon is encountered in the next stage of development in the Pauline communities.

The eschatological perspective of the Jesus movement does largely account for its inclusive attitudes towards women. Alongside the evidence of a passage like the one we quoted from Joel, there was the question of the role of the Jewish law which was the major restrictive influence on Jewish women's lives, particularly with the added element of Hellenistic influence. The prophet Jeremiah looked to a future utopia where people would by nature follow God's will, and he used the image of circumcision of the heart to depict this hope:

> The days are coming, says the Lord, when I will make a new covenant with the house of Israel and the house of Judah. It will not be like the covenant I made with their ancestors. . . . I will put my law within them, and I will write it on their hearts; and I will be their God, and they shall be my people. No longer shall they teach one another, or say to each other, 'Know the Lord,' for they shall all know me, from the least of them to the greatest, says the Lord; for I will forgive their iniquity; and remember their sin no more.
>
> (Jer. 31.31–34)

This concept potentially held immense promise for women's status in a Jewish context: the rite that recognized Jewish identity in a form that was exclusively restricted to men was now redefined in such a way that women could be included, on equal terms, beside men. The teaching contained here was particularly significant in the ministry of St Paul, who used this type of argument to explain why Gentiles might be admitted to the Christian communities without being circumcised.[230] In a context where the communities were already anticipating the fruits of the eschatological kingdom, the law did not apply in the same way as it had before the Messiah had appeared.[231] What we need to note is that there are crucial implications from this not only for would-be Gentile converts, but also for women's status within these communities.

The a-familial teaching of Jesus had some particularly challenging aspects for women, and here we are referring to those who literally followed Jesus, rather than those whose houses offered support *en route*. We know from the accounts of Jesus in Jerusalem at the time of his execution that there were women with him who had accompanied him from Galilee.[232] Is it the eschatological context of Jesus' ministry that explains why these women should behave in such an extraordinary way, to leave home and family and go 'on the road'? It would seem that fervent belief in the imminent close of history and the dawn of a new age would have been a significant factor. In addition we have to cast around the context of Judaism of that time to see if there is any phenomenon remotely similar that might add credibility to this explanation. In the previous section we did note one group described as the Therapeutrides: women who had opted out of family life, adopted celibacy and lived apart from mainstream society.[233] There were male counterparts, the Therapeutae, but they lived separately, and the two groups only came together, though without mingling, for weekly worship.[234] Although this phenomenon does not match the experience of female itinerant followers of Jesus, it does provide an interesting parallel, within Judaism, where women exercised some autonomy within a religious context. The celibate life allowed them an alternative to the usual pattern of domestic and family existence.

In her study of the Jesus movement Fiorenza points to an older literary source for supplementary evidence to explain in part the relatively enlightened attitude to women found in the earliest form of Christianity. The apocryphal *Book of Judith* is an important textual illustration for our period, which deserves our close attention. Written sometime between 163 and 142 BCE, during the Hasmonean period of Jewish history, by a Palestinian Jew, it tells the tale of a heroic female character, Judith, who intervened in a military campaign against a Jewish town. A recent commentator makes the following comment on the history of interpretation of the Judith narrative: 'Numerous images of Judith as femme fatale, civic patriot, precursor of Jesus, trickster, woman warrior, and a saviour in Israel, find their genesis in the Holofernes event, in which Judith assassinates an enemy general.'[235]

The first Christian writer to draw attention to this narrative was Clement of Rome who wrote of the 'blessed Judith', and observed that 'many women, empowered by God's grace, have performed deeds worthy of men' (1 Clem. 55.3.4). God is depicted by the author of the Judith narrative as, 'The God of the lowly, helper of the oppressed, upholder of the weak, protector of the forsaken, saviour of those without hope' (Jud. 9.11); that is, the same God identified in Jesus' ministry.

The story of Judith may be said to encapsulate two types of image of women found in Hebrew narrative: Ruth and Jael. The story is not intended to be historical, rather it is a story which epitomizes the struggles of Israel against her powerful neighbours, and this struggle she survives, despite her apparent weaknesses, because God is on her side. In the story Judith represents Israel: her name means literally 'Jewish woman'. The opposition is a composite mixture of Israel's traditional enemies the Assyrians and the Babylonians: history is suspended and Nebuchadnezzar is King of Assyria. His chief general and second in command is Holofernes. Holofernes is commanded to invade and conquer all the west country, that is, many small states including Israel. When Joakim, the high priest in Jerusalem, hears of Holofernes' plundering, he sends word to the people of Bethulia to secure the hill passes so that the invading armies cannot approach. Holofernes marches on the hilltowns, but, instead of confronting them in battle, he takes possession of their water supplies and decides to starve them out for daring to arm themselves against him. This is the point at which Judith enters the story: the personification of the valiant heart of powerless Israel. Like a lamb to the slaughter she offers to go, with God on her side, and do what is required for Israel. She succeeds and the nation is saved. What is interesting to us is the manner in which she achieves success.

In a recent study of Judith, Andre LaCocque notes that the story can be seen as: 'an anthology of texts about, and allusions to, other women in the Bible: Miriam, Deborah, Jael, Sarah, Rebecca, Rachel, Tamar, Naomi, Ruth, and Abigail'.[236] LaCocque refers to feminist scholars who see in Judith a transcending of the gender barriers but using female models, embodying both the soldier – *pace* Deborah and Jael; and the seductress – *pace* Tamar and Ruth. In her plan to save Israel her behaviour is first described in terms that are meant to recall the story of Ruth,[237] where, like Ruth, she is a young widow blatantly using her feminine wiles. Holofernes is not an attractive character; he is quite unlike Ruth's Boaz:

> Holofernes held a banquet for his personal attendants only, and did not invite any of his officers. He said to Bagoas, the eunuch who had charge of his personal affairs, 'Go, and persuade the Hebrew woman who is in your care to join us and to eat and drink with us. For it would be a disgrace if we let such a woman go without having intercourse with her. If we do not seduce her, she will laugh at us.'
>
> (12:10–12)

But the scene does recall Boaz's threshing floor where heavy drinking and feasting allow for the deception to occur (12.13–13.2).

Here, however, there is no seduction, only a very bloody murder for which Judith exchanges her guise of Ruth for that of Jael, the woman featured in the story of Deborah who strikes a tent-peg through the head of Sisera, the commander of the Canaanite army (Judges 4.4–5.31).

Judith is a character who behaves in a manner normally reserved in biblical narrative for men, and matched only by a woman of Jael's ruthlessness. Once Holofernes is in bed and overcome with wine, Judith stands up beside the bed, and calls upon God for strength (13.4–5), reminding the readers that what she does is done for the greater good of Israel. She then takes Holofernes' sword in one hand and his hair in another, calls upon God for strength once more, and hacks off his head with two blows of the sword. There is clear allusion to the David and Goliath story in *Judith*. Significantly, Judith does not accomplish her work with one blow as when David cuts off Goliath's head (1 Sam. 17.51). Also another biblical story is brought to mind where an unnamed 'wise woman' orders a decapitation for the sake of preserving the city of Abel (2 Sam. 20). As in the story of David and Goliath, where David is referred to as a 'stripling' (1 Sam. 17.56), in *Judith* the onlookers express wonder that a mighty warrior could be cut down by one so much weaker. Judith herself draws attention to the disparity between the victor and the vanquished: 'The Lord has struck him down by the hand of a woman' (Jud.13.15). The stark contrast between the woman who uses her body and the woman who uses her ruthlessness – between the 'Ruth' and the 'Jael' – comes out clearly in the Song of Judith:

> But the lord Almighty has foiled them by the hand of a woman. For the mighty one did not fall by the hands of the young men, nor did the hands of the Titans strike him down, nor did giants set upon him; but Judith daughter of Merari with the beauty of her countenance undid him. For she put away her widow's clothing to exalt the oppressed in Israel. She anointed her face with perfume; she fastened her hair with a tiara and put on a linen gown to beguile him. Her sandal ravished his eyes, her beauty captivated his mind, and the sword severed his neck! The Persians trembled at her boldness, the Medes were daunted at her daring.
>
> (16.5–10)

Although the story is a violent one, at its heart lies the belief in the god of the oppressed and hopeless. Although Judith uses very 'politically incorrect' strategies of deliberate seduction as the means to her end, this is noted by the narrative and turned upside down to reveal how Holofernes' assumptions about women, those of traditional patriarchal society, led to his death:

> And Holofernes said to her, 'God has done well to send you ahead of the people, to strengthen our hands and bring destruction on those who have despised my lord. You are not only beautiful in appearance, but wise in speech.'
>
> (Jud.11.22–23)

George Nickelsburg comments on the character of Judith as follows:

> Judith is no weakling. Her courage, her trust in God, and her wisdom – all lacking in her male counterparts – save the day for Israel. Her use of deceit and specifically of her sexuality may seem offensive and chauvinistic. For the author it is the opposite. Judith wisely chooses the weapon in her arsenal that is appropriate to her enemy's weakness. She plays his game, knowing that he will lose. In doing so she makes fools out of a whole army of men.[238]

For Fiorenza and other recent commentators on this period, *Judith* provides an important clue to the nature and context of Jesus' ministry which began not as a new religious movement but as a Jewish renewal movement, informed and inspired by the god revealed in Jewish scripture.

The main corpus of evidence for this stage are the letters written by Paul to various communities, 'the first urban Christians',[239] in the ancient cities which have survived through the centuries because they were preserved as Christian scripture in the canon. The letters of Paul are vital to our present study of women and Christianity since many of the comments relating to women found in them became authoritative in the lives of Christian women for two thousand years. Moreover, they have been instrumental in informing legal systems in western society on the status and rights of women, and forming the basis of women's status in all societies that have described themselves at some time as 'Christian'.

Paul entered the debate at a time when the urban communities were beginning to develop. He comes midpoint in the early development of Christianity, between the original eschatological itinerant Jesus movement, and the institutionalized church with its lack of eschatological dynamism and its comparatively well-developed hierarchy in the second century. As we saw in our opening description of early Christianity, the prophecies of the end-times were being taken literally, and these early communities did not seem to observe a sexual hierarchy, nor a preoccupation with the domestic versus the public, that is, a place for women and a place for men. The urban believers led a dual existence where, on the one hand, they followed their chosen professions or occupations accepting the existing social structures and behaviour of the world they lived in; while, on the other hand, they were part of a new age community when they met with their fellow believers. In this new community they anticipated God's kingdom where normal social structures were turned upside down, and the spirit reigned supreme. Gal. 3.28 is a baptismal formula dating from this period which epitomizes the new freedom experienced in the communities: 'There is neither Jew nor Greek, there is neither slave nor free, there is neither male nor female; for you are all one in Christ Jesus.'

We can see here similarities with the prophecy of Joel, noted earlier, both in sexual equality and status equality regarding servants and slaves. Paul characteristically extends the egalitarian utopia expressed in *Joel* further by giving it a universalism that includes Jews and Greeks side by side.[240]

The early Pauline letters, such as Romans, 1 and 2 Corinthians and Galatians, provide us with important evidence for the egalitarian nature of the early urban communities. The nature of the evidence is twofold, first, in terms of theological insights, such as the one we noted in Gal. 3.28; and, second, in terms of clues to the social ranks and occupations of the individuals mentioned by name, particularly in the greetings sections of these epistles.

The egalitarian attitude and theology expressed in Gal. 3.28 can also be found in 1 Cor. 7 where Paul advised the community on marriage in the light of the Christ event:

> the wife does not have authority over her own body, but the husband does; likewise the husband does not have authority over his own body, but the wife does. . . . To the unmarried and the widows I say it is well for them to remain unmarried as I am. But if they are not practising self-control, they should marry. For it is better to marry than to be aflame with passion.
>
> (1 Cor. 7.4 and 8–9)

Here Paul begins his excursus on marriage by showing that there should be parity between male and female, at least in terms of conjugal rights. Both men and women lose their autonomy over their bodies when they marry. In Paul's understanding marriage was a radical change of circumstances from the single state for both parties. If they were part of the new age, then, he questioned whether marriage was the best state to be in for those unique and challenging times. The community might have been better served by the single-mindedness of the unmarried state. He recognized that if this single state was involuntary, then the advantage of being single was lost since that individual would be consumed by the need for sexual fulfilment. This view he underlined again later in the chapter:

> Now concerning virgins, I have no command of the Lord, but I give my opinion as one who by the Lord's mercy is trust-worthy. I think that in view of the impending crisis it is well for you to remain as you are. Are you bound to a wife? Do not seek to be free. Are you free from a wife? Do not seek a wife. But if you marry, you do not sin, and if a virgin marries, she does not sin.
>
> (7.25–28a)

Here Paul becomes apocalyptic in his language to urge the community to remember the eschatological nature of the times they were living in:

> Yet those who are married will experience distress in this life, and I would spare you that. I mean, brothers and sisters, the appointed time has grown short; from now on, let even those who have wives be as though they had none, and those who mourn as though they were not mourning, and those who rejoice as though they were not rejoicing, and those who buy as though they had no possessions, and those who deal with the world as though they had no dealings with it. For the present form of this world is passing away.
>
> (7.28b–31)

A sideways glance at other scriptural passages describing family relations at the time of divine judgement in apocalyptic terms set Paul's concerns expressed here in perspective:

> for nation will rise against nation, and kingdom against king-dom; there will be earthquakes in various places; there will

be famines. This is but the beginning of the birthpangs. . . .
Brother will betray brother to death, and a father his child, and
children will rise against parents and have them put to death.

(Mk 13.8 and 12)

This is what Paul would have spared his community: the agony of
familial separation and suffering that would have inevitably occurred
at the time of judgement, a time that Paul was convinced would come
in the near future.

Paul's teaching on marriage in the context of that eschatological
community remains consistent with the baptismal formula quoted in
Gal. 3.28. Marriage, when it did occur for the believer, should be a
relationship of mutual respect and mutual rights. His ambivalence
came from his fear that such concern to be a good partner would
inevitably distract from a focus on Christ and his imminent return,
and then store up potential future suffering when some family ties
would be violently broken at the eschaton.

According to comments in the Corinthian and Galatian correspondence, women seem to have been given at least notional equal
status within the communities. We need to ask now if there were any
practical applications of their new status, for example, in a liturgical
context. 1 Cor. 11 seems to suggest that women were accorded the
same roles in the public worship as men, although, at the same time,
many controversial issues are raised regarding gender roles:

I commend you because you remember me in everything and
maintain the traditions just as I handed them onto you. But I
want you to understand that Christ is the head of every man,
and the husband is the head of his wife, and God is the head of
Christ. Any man who prays or prophesies with something on
his head disgraces his head, but any woman who prays or
prophesies with her head unveiled disgraces her head – it is one
and the same thing as having her head shaved.

(11.2–5)

It would seem that the Corinthian women had displeased Paul by
exercising their ministries at community gatherings with their heads
uncovered, but his emotive words concerning women's head-dress
should not be allowed to obscure the fact that women *were* exercising
ministries, that is to say, they were active participants in that
liturgical context.

This is a chapter that has attracted immense attention from the time of the first century to the present day. Fiorenza notes that debate concerning Paul's comments on women's head covering usually focuses on whether women should be veiled, noting Jewish customs for women's dress. But, as she points out, Paul's focus is on the hair itself, and the point that Paul is making therefore concerns the manner in which hair is arranged while people are praying and prophesying:

> It seems that during their ecstatic-pneumatic worship celebrations some of the Corinthian women prophets and liturgists unbound their hair, letting it flow freely rather than keeping it in its fashionable coiffure, which often was quite elaborate and enhanced with jewelry, ribbons and veils. Such a sight of disheveled hair would have been quite common in the ecstatic worship of oriental deities.[241]

The classical scholar Balsdon comments on the complex hair-styles current in the Empire during the first century CE, and cites Julia the daughter of Titus, who became Emperor in 79 CE, as being a notorious trend-setter in coiffure, and notes the satirist Juvenal's mocking comments on the practice:

> Curl climbs on top of curl and over the forehead there arose something which at its best looked like the *chef d'oeuvre* of a gifted pastrycook and, at its worst, like a dry sponge. At the back the hair was plaited, and the braids arranged in a coil which looks like basketwork. The towering splendour was to be viewed from one direction only, the front, and women must have manoevered at social gatherings, to keep out of view the ridiculous anti-climax which the backs of their hair constituted. 'Storey and storey are built up on her lofty head. See her from in front; she is Andromache. From behind she looks half the size – a different woman, you would think.' So Juvenal mocked (Juv. 6, 502–4).[242]

Although such extremely elaborate hairdressing belonged to the social world of the imperial household, the fashion was generally for women to wear their long hair firmly bound up in attractive coils and plaits. To undress it so that it hung loose could not have been a casual movement, but a deliberate gesture.

Paul later in this section of his letter to Corinth deals with the need for order and decency in community worship (Chapters 11–14), and he makes it clear that his primary concern lies with the situation an outsider would find if they entered such a gathering for the first time: 'will they not say that you are out of your mind?' (14.23). Fiorenza notes a tension between Paul and the Corinthians regarding the image they projected in the ancient city. Whereas the Corinthians were content to emulate and merge in with popular oriental-style religions, Paul wanted to distinguish early Christianity from them. The debate on women's hair is a focus for this general tension. Women who took part in the worship of Isis let their hair flow loose, a practice noted by the early first-century CE Roman poet Tibullus who mentions a woman untying her hair twice daily to praise Isis.[243] Similar practice occurred among the maenads of Dionysian devotion, and the women worshippers of Cybele (Magna Mater). In the case of Isis, the men would shave their heads, and here Fiorenza finds a possible explanation for Paul's comment that women may as well shave their heads. We might also mention the male priests, the *galli*, of the Magna Mater cult who, as well as castrating themselves, wore women's clothes and their hair hung long and loose.[244] The male and female characteristics were being blurred to the point of indecency in Paul's eyes. Gender boundaries were being crossed. To a Jew by birth and practice, the other oriental cults were idolatrous and immoral, an affront to the one and true God. To observe practices among communities that he had founded himself that were making them indistinguishable from paganism would have upset Paul, and this helps us explain the emotion and condemnation in this chapter.[245]

. Other evidence for the practical involvement of women in the early urban communities comes to us through the individuals named by Paul in his letters. In his letter to Rome he mentions Phoebe, a deacon, 'that you may welcome her in the Lord as is fitting for the saints, and help her in whatever she may require from you, for she has been a benefactor of many and of myself as well' (16.1–2); he greets the couple Prisca and Aquila, 'who work with me in Christ Jesus' (16.3); and he mentions Junia as a fellow apostle (16.6).[246] The *Acts of the Apostles* mentions a convert of Paul named Lydia (16.14–15), who had her own business dyeing purple. She was a wealthy businesswoman who was able to offer her home and household to the apostles. These are some of the women we know existed and held important positions in terms of support and organization in the early urban communities.[247] There is a temptation to compare these women with those individuals discussed by Bernadette Brooten in her research on the inscriptions that refer to women holding prominent positions in some of the ancient synagogues.[248]

Both groups were wealthy women with the resources to support their adopted or native religious community.

Whilst we can uncover an egalitarian type of community organization from the evidence of the early Pauline letters, we do also discover a tension. This can be explained, at least in part, by taking into account the middle stage in the development of first-century Christianity which Paul occupies. His communities still enjoy the 'fruits of the spirit', and fixed organizational structures are invisible. There is only the charismatic church (1 Cor. 12), where the spirit stands in place of any hierarchy, and all are equal members of Christ's body: the church. These were eschatological communities, awaiting the imminent return of Christ, and holding out against the standards and structures of their age. However, as time was passing, the sense of Christ's imminent return began to diminish. It became increasingly difficult to withstand the pressures to conform to external influences in the communities' own organization and attitudes. The Corinthian correspondence monitors this tension. Attitudes to women and their participation within the communities were a focus for it, as we have seen in the incident concerning hair-style. Thus we have an ambivalent picture emerging of the position of women in these early urban communities. On the one hand there was a continuation of eschatological zeal from the Jesus movement, based on the liberating experience of the free spirit; whilst on the other hand, a theological argument and practice began to emerge restoring women to the status of the second sex.

Following on from the Jesus movement, we find in Paul's urban communities charismatic leadership where the barriers between men and women were broken down; all were children of God blessed by his spirit, and called to various offices irrespective of their gender. Marriage was not encouraged unless celibacy was causing the 'flesh' to dominate a particular individual. The ideal was an individual, male or female, who was single-mindedly dedicated to God in the light of the gospel of Christ, and in expectation of the imminent return of Christ and the judgement of the present order. There was a role for celibate women in the church, women who were not distracted by domestic concerns, who like Judith preferred a life dedicated to God to a life of marriage and domesticity: 'For the rest of her life she was honoured throughout the whole country. Many desired to marry her, but she gave herself to no man all the days of her life' (Jud. 16.21–22).

The tension we noted in the communities addressed by the Pauline correspondence heightened as the first century progressed. The pressure to create more structures for ease of communication and decision making was not always resisted. A community run on charismatic principles could lead to distrust and a type of spiritual conceit that, paradoxically, created a hierarchy of charisma. Such problems were already noted by Paul who encouraged the Corinthians to engage their minds as well as their gifts of the spirit:

> I will pray with the spirit, but I will pray with the mind also; I will sing praise with the spirit, but I will sing praise with the mind also. Otherwise if you say a blessing with the spirit, how can anyone in the position of an outsider say the 'Amen' to your thanksgiving, since the outsider does not know what you are saying?
>
> (1 Cor. 14.15–16)

Here again we see Paul's concern about the 'outsider', a self-consciousness as to how his communities were being perceived in the 'outside' world. With the advent of persecution, notably sporadic and spontaneous, but also systematic as at the time of Nero,[249] this self-consciousness intensified. Their appearance to the world outside became a crucial consideration for the very existence of many communities. Coupled with this pressure was the internal factor of the non-occurrence of God's judgement and non-return of the Messiah. Instead of a self-awareness of being a millenarian set of believers, eagerly awaiting the end-time, the early Christians had to face up to the prospect of long-term existence in 'this world'. Biblical texts dating from the end of the first century reflect such tendencies clearly.[250] The status of women within the communities became a central issue for communities that had to develop hierarchical structures for organization. The tradition of women who set aside marriage and family for the sake of the gospel continued in Christianity, but became marginalized as a form of leadership. Fiorenza comments on the complexity of the situation as Christianity developed into the second century CE:

> Patriarchalization of the early Christian movement and ascendency of the monarchical episcopacy not only made marginal or excluded women leaders in the early church but also segregated and restricted them to women's spheres, which gradually came under the control of the bishop. Nevertheless, it must be emphasized again that the writings suggesting this kind of

patriarchal dynamic are *prescriptive* rather than *descriptive*, since the male clergy were often dependent upon wealthy and influential women even into late antiquity. Ideological prescription and actual social reality do not always correspond.[251]

This is a crucial point which makes sense of discrepancies and the pluralism of Christian practice during those early years. We have passages that give clear instruction for the marginalization of women from church offices:

> also that the women should dress themselves modestly and decently in suitable clothing, not with their hair braided, or with gold, pearls, or expensive clothes, but with good works, as is proper for women who profess reverence for God. Let a woman learn in silence with full submission. I permit no woman to teach or to have authority over a man; she is to keep silent.
>
> (1 Tim. 29.12)[252]

This evidence on its own points to the existence of practices to the contrary: otherwise such a prohibition would not be needed. But the popular Montanist movement of the second century provides further evidence.[253] The Montanists were a mid-second-century millenarian movement in Phrygia in Asia Minor, inspired and led by the prophecies of a man and two women: Montanus, and Prisca and Maximilla. They had a significant following, including the church father Tertullian. The movement actually caused a schism in Asia Minor, and despite apparent victory by the anti-Montanists, followers of the sect lived on. The controversy actually prompted the formalization of the New Testament canon, such was the fear that the new prophecies might have been included. Thus into the second century we find women led by the spirit, in turn, leading Christian communities. One of the problems for prevailing Christianity at that time was the high-profile female leadership of the Montanist movement. Movements such as Montanism made Christianity seem far from respectable, and its message concerning the imminent return of Christ was not popular in the developing institutionalized Christianity. Its eventual marginalization from the mainstream, or emerging Christian orthodoxy, is not therefore surprising. It is important to note that in early Christianity there was a link between female leadership and imminent eschatology. It would seem that female authority could be accepted and acclaimed for an interim period when history was about to come to an end. When Christianity began looking to the long term then conventional male leadership and hierarchy became normative.

Another example of a famous female celibate at the end of the New Testament period is Thecla. Her story is found in an apocryphal book, the *Acts of Paul and Thecla*,[254] and it is told in a romantic narrative dating from the same period as the Montanist movement, which also came from Asia Minor. It is set in the time of Paul's ministry, and like the Jewish epic of Judith, is more fiction than fact, but, like Judith, provides a useful piece of evidence for alternative models for women in the early church. Thecla was a beautiful young virgin who renounced a lucrative marriage, cut off her hair and dressed in men's clothes. She ran away from home to embark on a ministry of preaching, basing her life on Paul's teaching of the virgin life. These measures were to avoid being raped, a fate she narrowly escaped by the timely intervention of a miraculous storm cloud. Although Thecla's story was marginalized by the western church, she is revered as a saint by the eastern church.

Despite attempts to restrict women in terms of their active and visible participation in Christianity their contributions continued into the second century. We have noted the comment from 1 Timothy forbidding women to hold positions of authority over men, and we need to mention in the same context the restrictions that same text placed on the widows in the community. A reference to *real widows* (1 Tim. 5) implies that there was some debate about the nature of widowhood. The text states that a woman can be classed as a widow only if she is over 60 years of age. Requirements for their enrolment in the communities resemble those for a bishop (1 Tim. 5.3–16), and we are told that only 'real' widows deserved the support of the community, that is, those with no surviving family. This is despite the fact that these widows were employed in the service of the community, in much the same way as male elders and bishops whose remuneration was not dependent on family means but on their ability to contribute to the up-building of the community. Furthermore, the male office bearers received pay double that of the widows.

Another point to note in relation to a widow's age requirement of 60 given in the Pastorals (a collective term for the New Testament epistles 1 Timothy, 2 Timothy and Titus) related to a requirement in Roman legislation introduced by Augustus.[255] This law arose in the context of an alarming drop in the birth rate coupled with the need to maintain high numbers in the militia. Widows who wished to remain unmarried after the death of their husbands should be 50 or 60 years of age, that is, past child-bearing age. The Pastorals advise that younger widows be discouraged from joining the order of widows in case at a later time they wish to remarry. Consciously or unconsciously, the option for younger women to remain single was being made difficult, in stark contrast to Paul's encouragement to young women to remain single (1 Cor. 7.39). In practice it would seem that in the early church the order of widows was a community of women of all ages committed to serving their Lord in the ways encouraged by Paul. Further evidence for this comes from the second century CE, from Ignatius of Antioch who in his *Letter to the Smyrnaeans* greets the order of widows as 'virgins who call themselves widows' (13.1). By restricting the order of widows to women over 60 this alternative Christian community or household would be curtailed, and women would no longer have the option, as they had in the time of Paul and the other apostles, to live lives independent of the domestic realm. In the ideal offered by 1 Timothy, and its associated texts 2 Timothy and Titus, women had to marry and bear children, and they could only opt out of that once they had fulfilled their domestic duties. We must remember, once again, that for the author of the Pastorals to have mentioned these widows and to have prescribed an age limit and behaviour type for them must indicate that this was not how they were behaving. Fiorenza argues that the order of widows was an important means by which young women were able to avoid marriage and the attentions of men. By declaring themselves 'widows' they took up a style of dress and life that removed them from the usual expectations, and allowed them to exercise freedom in terms of working within and for the community.[256] The disapproval voiced against women who chose this life could stem from fear of repercussions if Christianity challenged the norms of social behaviour. Additionally, we could have evidence here of Hellenistic influence on the embryonic church. As we shall see there are biblical texts that reiterate the norms for gender roles from Hellenistic sources: the 'household codes' in Colossians, Ephesians and 1 Peter bear a striking similarity to the philosophical ideas of Aristotle.[257]

Lying at the heart of the contrast between an egalitarian community and hierarchical patriarchy are two polarized attitudes to the family. Both are found in Christian scripture, and both can be traced throughout Christianity's history. First, we have the attitude outlined above in our discussion of the Jesus movement where followers were encouraged to leave homes and family and become members of the community: the family of God. Thus traditional familial ties are broken and sisters in Christ are free to live and work in the public sphere alongside men. Second, there are the household codes. These codes offer a sexual hierarchy, with the husband's headship reflecting that of Christ's headship of the church. When we look at comparable Greco-Roman household codes we see that these epistles have simply adopted a common social structure from Greco-Roman society and given it a theological foundation. Recently scholars have recognized a parallel in the treatises on economics and politics which reflect a form already codified by Aristotle, and this form was common in philosophical schools of the first century CE. In these codes the aim was to reinforce subordination within the patriarchal family on the one hand; and on the other to incorporate the ideals of mutual support formulated in the Hellenistic age. Fiorenza discusses the various types of household codes from the ancient world and she notes: 'in antiquity the household was economically independent, self-sufficient, hierarchically ordered, and as such the basis of the state.'[258]

Aristotle sees the family as the basis, the perfect paradigm, for politics and the state. He describes the family in the following terms of natural ruler and natural subject. The addition of slaves turns a family into a household. Many households make a village, several villages a city state or *politeia*. This way Aristotle illustrates how the family forms the very basis of the state. As such it must in essence embody the necessary structure that will form the basis of society within the state, namely that of a patriarchal hierarchy reflecting the correlation of natural ruler and natural subject:

> there are by nature various classes of rulers and ruled. For the free rules the slave, the male the female, the man the child in a different way. And all possess the various parts of the soul but possess them in different ways; for the slave has not got the deliberative part at all, and the female has it but without full authority, while the child has it but in an undeveloped form.
>
> (*Politics* I.1260a)

Most critics today recognize the negative influence that Aristotle had on Christianity regarding his belief that women represented defective humanity.[259] What has not been so readily noted, as Fiorenza points out,[260] is how this anthropology is actually rooted in his thinking on the state and politics. His idea that female nature was such as to be unfit to rule was not universally held in his own day. In Sparta, for example, women controlled their own wealth and therefore held significant power as a result.[261] Also Plato suggested that granted equal opportunity, women could hold the same offices as men.[262] Aristotle's model for the family and state in his own day was only an alternative, and not the natural order of things as he maintained.

Aristotle's influence on Christianity cannot be overestimated. It would be misleading to think it is only evident in the work of Augustine and Aquinas – extensive though that is. He indirectly influenced Christianity from the time of its earliest origins. At the very beginnings of Christianity Aristotle's thought was undergoing a renaissance in both neo-Pythagorean philosophy and stoic philosophy. In Hellenistic Judaism we also find evidence of its influence,[263] lying behind, for example, the picture of the good wife and the bad wife described in the Egyptian Jewish Hellenistic apocryphal work *Sirach* (25.16–26.4). The dire picture of the bad wife keeping possession of her wealth and thus threatening the whole institution of the family comes close to the tone of Aristotle's attack on Spartan culture. We should note also in the passage from *Sirach* a theological underpinning for basic Aristotelian patriarchy, vs 24, underlining the in-built character defect of the female sex.[264]

The earliest household code of Christian scripture is thought to be that found in Colossians:

> Wives, be subject to your husbands, as is fitting in the Lord. Husbands, love your wives and never treat them harshly. Children, obey your parents in everything, for this is your acceptable duty in the Lord. Fathers, do not provoke your children, or they may lose heart. Slaves, obey your earthly masters in everything, not only while being watched, and in order to please them, but wholeheartedly, fearing the Lord. . . . Masters, treat your slaves justly and fairly, for you know that you also have a Master in heaven.
>
> (Col. 3.20–22 and 4.1)

As Fiorenza notes, this household power structure revolves around three pairs: wife/husband; children/father; slave/master: 'In each case, the socially subordinate first member of the pair is exhorted to obedience to the superordinate second'.[265] The Christian element in the household code is focused on the phrase 'in the Lord', which suffices as an explanation for the structure. It is the will of the deity.

When we turn to the household code in 1 Peter 2.11–3.12 we discover one of the three pairs noted in Colossians to be missing, that of children and parents. Also, it stresses the duties of the subordinate party rather than the superordinate party:

> For the Lord's sake accept the authority of every human institution, whether of the emperor as supreme, or of governors, as sent by him to punish those who do wrong and to praise those who do right.... As servants of God, live as free people, yet do not use your freedom as a pretext for evil. Honour everyone. Love the family of believers. Fear God. Honour the emperor. Slaves accept the authority of your masters with all deference, not only those who are kind and gentle, but also those who are harsh.
>
> (1 Peter 2.13–14, 16–18)

As this code of behaviour continues, the ideal behavioural pattern for slaves is applied to wives:

> Wives, in the same way, accept the authority of your husbands.... Do not adorn yourselves outwardly by braiding your hair, and by wearing gold ornaments or fine clothing; rather, let your adornment be the inner self with the lasting beauty of a gentle and quiet spirit, which is very precious in God's sight.
>
> (1 Peter 3.1a and 3–4)

In this structure, state, household, family, we find a type of code closely reflecting Aristotle's *politeia*.[266] Fiorenza comments that this example of a household code, with its patriarchal pattern of submission, 'does not so much seek to put wives back into their proper patriarchal roles and places, but seeks to lessen the tension between the Christian community and the pagan patriarchal household'.[267] Using evidence from ancient texts, including the second-century Christian heretic Marcion who noted that Jesus himself had been charged with leading astray women and children, Fiorenza stresses the political threat Christian egalitarian values could have posed to the Roman state. With teaching characterized by an option for women and other disempowered strata of society, the early promises of the Jesus movement were undermining the political basis of Roman society, the family and the recognized status of slaves.

In those three household codes we can see how patriarchal order is introduced into the Christian household. When we turn to the

Pastorals once more we can find the introduction of patriarchal order into the church and ministry as well. These epistles give instructions concerning behaviour in the household of God (1 Tim. 3.15). The head of this household is the bishop, sometimes translated 'overseer'. The model for his (*sic*) behaviour is outlined in 1 Timothy:

> whoever aspires to the office of bishop desires a noble task. Now a bishop must be above reproach, married only once, temperate, sensible, respectable, hospitable, an apt teacher, not a drunkard, not violent but gentle, not quarrelsome, and not a lover of money. He must manage his own household well, keeping his children submissive and respectful in every way – for if someone does not know how to manage his own household, how can he take care of God's church?
>
> (1 Tim. 3.1–5) (also, Tit. 1.7ff.)

Just as wives (Tit. 2.5), children (1 Tim. 3.4) and slaves (Tit. 2.9), must be submissive in the household, so they must be submissive in the community. A wife/woman is to be totally submissive to a husband/man (1 Tim. 2.10–15). Just as slaves must not have contempt for their masters (1 Tim. 6.2), so the whole community should not have contempt for its ministers (1 Tim. 4.12; Tit. 2.15). The overall message of the Pastorals is that Christians should be model citizens in their households and worshipping communities. They observe the patriarchal order and pray for 'emperors and all authorities' and 'lead a quiet and peaceful life in all piety and dignity' (1 Tim. 2.1ff.).

Here we see another change in direction for Christian life, in addition to marriage and the household. Now ministry too is dependent on age and gender qualifications, not as previously recognized (e.g. 1 Cor. 12–14) on a person's spiritual or organizational resources or gifts. Tit. 2.3–5 mentions women teachers which seems to contradict 1 Tim. 2.10, but this is not the case when we realize that their role is restricted to teaching other women.

This is the picture then at the end of the New Testament period and at the end of the first century of the Christian era. As far as the later texts are concerned, Christianity has become a patriarchal religion, inspired by and reflecting the patriarchal nature of the society it exists in.

By the end of the early formative period of Christianity, that is by the beginning of the second century CE, we can see an independent religion emerging that is syncretized with the Roman state. Its patterns for private and public behaviour and structures are a mirror reflection of the ideals for a settled political environment for the rule of the Empire. Christianity did not challenge the state, rather, it encouraged its adherents to be model citizens. This encouragement was enriched by the claim that the prescribed code of conduct was God's will and by promises of heavenly rewards. Such a picture is one that is in striking contrast to the aims and lifestyle of the Jesus movement. There an egalitarian rather than hierarchical model was described, and there activities and tasks were assigned to individuals by God's spirit, regardless of their gender or background. We should avoid the temptation to account for this contrast in simple terms of historical development. These paradigms for behaviour and organization appear in texts that are not significantly distanced by time. For example, Colossians, which contains a household code, cannot be dated plausibly later than about 60 CE, a mere five or so years after 1 Corinthians. Diversity of practice would be a more convincing explanation, and this diversity can be explained if we take account of the fact that certain communities were under threat of persecution, while others faced the influence of local pagan shrines. Factors such as these affect the way in which a particular community presented itself to the outside world, or strengthened itself internally.

It is the interpretation and application of these texts in the history of Christianity that is significant for women. Diversity, and therefore the inclusion of women at all levels within that religion, could continue as long as heterodoxy was tolerated. Many factors contributed to the loss of diversity within Christianity from the second century onwards, and by the end of that century there is a clearly discernible notion of orthodoxy with a canon of scripture to support it. Women's role diminished with the rise of orthodoxy, and teaching on women outlined in the Pastorals and the household codes became normative. Those are the texts constantly quoted by the church fathers from the second century on, while those that offer alternative options for women are rarely discussed.[268]

Christianity in these early centuries was prescriptive in relation to women. In effect it constructed their gender by explaining to them what it meant to be a woman. It declared what women should look like: how they should wear their hair, the type of clothes that are suitable, whether they should wear jewellery. It presumed that they would marry and have children, and having achieved this, at the end of their lives they would become widows, and then they were told how they should give their services to the church. In our next section we will explore in more depth the way in which Christian theology underpins these prescriptions and works out a psychological dimension for this role provision.

In our survey of women in Greco-Roman religion, Judaism and Christianity we have noted such a degree of diversity that any comparative generalizations would be meaningless. It is the diversity itself that demands our attention, something that is often lost in studies of religion in this period. Paganism, Judaism and Christianity are far from homogeneous, and we have noted a spectrum of diversity in all three. The vast array of religions in the Roman Empire meant cross-influences between traditions and cults: Greek religion becomes Roman, Persian beliefs become Jewish, Judaism becomes Christianity. In this complex and infinitely varied religious matrix women's experience is correspondingly diverse, ranging from being excluded entirely from public worship to full inclusion. In early Christian evidence women appear as sisters in Christ *and* daughters of Eve – the woman created to help and obey her husband. The rise of Christian orthodoxy together with the eventual conversion of the Emperor to Christianity, would lead inevitably to a radical narrowing of religious experience for all in the Roman world, with particular implications for women.

Part III

RELIGION AND GENDER

The previous two sections of this book have hinted at and sometimes explicitly engaged with the question of religion's role in the construction of gender. Notions of womanhood are put together through religious belief and practice, as well as through the legislative and cultural articulations of society. When a religion includes a powerful legislative and cultural heritage, as in the case of Judaism, then the religious influence on the construction of gender roles is all the more powerful. We noted in Judaism how the religious dimension pervades all aspects of life from the most public to the most private. Christianity, reflecting the intrusive nature of its parent religion, feels confident to advise on marriage, children, dress, coiffure and sexual activity. Both Judaism and Christianity offer total systems that encompass not only religious belief and religious ritual but a whole lifestyle. Unlike the majority of religions in the Greco-Roman world, Judaism and Christianity included moral codes that trespassed from the public sphere into the private. But in this respect they were not unique. Religion as a synthesis of moral code, faith in a divinity and hope for an afterlife can also be discerned in the development of at least two of the oriental cults in the Roman world, namely, those of Isis and Mithras, and it is useful to set Judaism and Christianity beside such cults within the Greco-Roman religious spectrum.

These more intrusive religions are inevitably more prescriptive for the lives of men and women. Obviously there were other factors that affected their lives at a more fundamental level: whether an individual was freeborn or a slave, whether they were rich or poor, whether or not they possessed Roman citizenship. Nonetheless such factors cannot always be distinguished from the religious sphere. If, for example, you were a slave belonging to a particular household whose head converted to Christianity, then you were also baptized (Acts 16.15), and became subject to the beliefs and disciplines of that religion. If you were a slave girl whose mistress became initiated into the Dionysus mysteries, then you accompanied her and were subject to the same code of secrecy.[269] It would be an artificial and unconvincing exercise to analyse the influence of religion on the articulation and construction of gender roles in isolation from other factors that inculturalize and socialize individuals. Religion is most useful as a tool that gauges the standards, practices and beliefs of society and culture. As such it reflects reality in a manner that is useful to sociologists, anthropologists and historians. Furthermore, it is an invaluable resource for reconstructing and tracing the development of gender constructs as they have appeared in the history of our civilization.

This then will be the focus of the third part of our analysis. We have described many of the features of women's roles in the societies of the Greco-Roman world, and discussed how those roles were translated into participation in the various types of religion present in that world. Up to this point we have been working only with the reflected image given by the mirror that is the broad spectrum of articulated religious experience in the ancient world. Our next step is to deconstruct the mirror itself in order to discover how the various concepts of womanhood reflected in the ancient religions are constructed.

We cannot raise the question of the construction of women's roles, or even the construction of the female gender itself, without engaging with the issue of its counterpart, maleness. When a patriarchal religion or society develops a strong and definitive notion of womanhood, that notion of the female tends to be formulated to confirm what it is not to be female. In other words womanhood became the 'other' in order to confirm the normative and primary concept of manhood.[270] This may not apply to all varieties of Greco-Roman culture prior to and apart from the Christian experience. But in an atmosphere of intensified dualism, such as that experienced in Christianity from the second century to the present day, the development of gender identity in terms of the male being normative and the female being derivative, or even defective, is clearly discernible.

7

MAGNA MATER AND THE VESTAL VIRGINS

Two examples from Greco-Roman religion provide tantalizing material for any discussion of the question of gender. The cults of Vesta and Magna Mater, or Cybele, both explode the conventions of gender expectation. The former is characterized by the Vestal Virgins,[271] who in various ways are perceived as men, and the latter by self-castrating eunuchs, the *galli*. The cult of Magna Mater, however, is an appropriate one to begin with as the goddess herself acquired such prominence in Roman culture. Even with the limited information we possess concerning her cult, we can create a convincing picture of at least one anti-type of idealized manhood.

In 204 BCE, according to Livy,[272] the cult of Magna Mater was introduced into Roman religious experience, from her native Pessinus in Asia Minor. As was the practice in the case of 'foreign' cults, it was given legal status in Rome through recourse to the Sibylline books.[273] Mary Beard notes two distinctive features in the Magna Mater cult as it appeared in Roman religious life.[274] In the first place it was characterized by an unusual emphasis on its ecstatic worship. But more significantly, it was a cult traditionally associated with the city of Troy, to which the origin of the Roman race was traced, and therefore could be regarded almost as an ancient Roman religion, rather than a new or foreign phenomenon. In Rome an image of Magna Mater, made out of a black meteorite, was set up in the heart of the city, in a temple on the Palatine Hill. In the mind of the poet Ovid, writing in the late first century BCE, the goddess had come 'home' to share life with other descendants of Troy in their new homeland in Italy.[275]

Suetonius records an incident supposed to have taken place in 204 BCE while the goddess was being taken up the River Tiber to Rome. The legend describes how the barge carrying the statue of Magna

Mater ran aground, and a young Roman heroine by the name of Quinta Claudia, using her own hair as a barge rope, intervened to tow the statue to its destination on the Palatine.[276] Claudia, who was suspected of unchastity at the time, threw herself on the mercy of the goddess pleading that her innocence had been proved by the intervention of the goddess who gave her the strength to tow the barge.

The commentators do not include any consort for Magna Mater in the earliest accounts, and, as a result, the male figure most closely associated with her, the god Attis, seems to have been a secondary feature of the cult, although there is archaeological evidence from the Palatine Hill which suggests that Attis was part of the cult from its earliest manifestation in Rome.[277] However that may be, the myth of Attis provides the basis for one of the most obvious cultic practices associated with the Magna Mater cult, namely the self-emasculation of her priests. The central theme of the many and varied legends describing Attis' relationship with Magna Mater focuses on the young mortal Attis, caught up in an ecstatic frenzy instigated by the goddess because she was jealous of his relationship with another woman. When, in this frenzy, Attis castrates himself and dies, the goddess herself brings him back to life.

Another ritual re-enacts the death and resurrection of Attis. Beard offers a tentative reconstruction of this ritual, based on a variety of types of evidence, often deliberately written to ridicule the practice it describes. The annual Magna Mater ritual took place during the period of 15 to 27 March, and seems to follow an established pattern from about the end of the second century CE. The ritual most closely associated with Attis was performed between 22 and 25 March. On 22 March the priests and other cult officials cut down a pine tree, beating their breasts in mourning, and carried it in a mock funeral procession across the city to the temple on the Palatine Hill. On the tree was an image of Attis who was said to have died under a pine tree after he had castrated himself. In some versions of the myth, he was eventually granted immortality in the form of a pine tree.[278] Beard reconstructs the next stage of the ritual as follows:

> The festival on 24 March (the day of blood) was marked, as its name suggests, by the shedding of human blood in the temple precinct. The priests and other worshippers tore their flesh with whips and pierced their breasts with the pine needles, sprinkling the blood on the tree and on the altars of the

precinct. It may also have been on this day that the would-be priest castrated himself, becoming a 'living Attis'. At some point during these proceedings, the pine tree was buried. On the next day (the day of joy), the resurrection of the god was celebrated.[279]

A more infamous aspect of the Magna Mater cult, performed during the March celebrations as well as at other times, was the *taurobolium*, the killing of a bull. This was a particularly gory practice where the animal was sacrificed in such a way as to ensure that the sacrificer was spattered with its blood. Beard notes how this distinguishes Magna Mater sacrifice from the normal cultic practice of Roman religion which was designed to ensure precisely the opposite effect, that the priest remained unstained throughout the ritual killing.[280] It must be admitted that the most gruesome account of this sacrifice stems from a piece of Christian polemic that describes how the officiating priest stood in a pit underneath the animal actually to be bathed in its blood.[281]

Other annual events included the *Megalensia*, exuberant festivities held in April to commemorate the arrival of the goddess in Rome with plays performed in front of the temple, circus events, and the like. During the festival the eunuch priests roamed through the city begging for alms, another practice which reverses normal Roman custom. Those holding priestly offices in the various civic cults were invariably prosperous and respected citizens who regularly used their office as a platform to display their *largesse* to those of lower social status.[282] Begging would have been a practice never contemplated by Roman civic priests.

The most intriguing feature of the Magna Mater cult is inevitably the self-castration of the *galli*. As Beard points out, the debate as to whether this actually happened historically and, if it did, to what degree they mutilated their genitals, is of less significance than the prominence this practice is given in Roman imagination. Beard sees here evidence for the tendency of Roman society to distance itself from the Magna Mater cult, and name it and its accompanying practices as the 'other': 'it is an insistence on distance and difference, particularly focused on the eunuch galli'.[283]

In the context of gender construction, the image of the Magna Mater cult with its eunuch priests provides an example of what maleness should not be, thus reinforcing the accepted norms of what it should be. In Roman terms, 'the eunuch gallus was both a non-man and a man who broke the rules of proper male behaviour'.[284] The *galli* were not only emasculated by self-mutilation, but apparently also by wearing women's clothes and having long hair. Beard's article cites an epigram written by the Roman poet Martial in the second half of the first century CE which ridicules the sexual ambiguity of the *galli*:

> What, licking women down inside there, Gallus?
> The thing you should be sucking is a phallus.
> They cut your cock off, but not so to bed,
> Cunt-lover: what needs doctoring now's your head.
> For while your missing member can't but fail,
> Your tongue still breaks Cybele's rule: it's male.[285]

The effeminate appearance of the *galli* would normally signal an attraction to men. To be sexually attractive *as* men was to upset the gender balance as understood by Roman society.

The elite custodians of Roman standards provide a critique of the imported oriental cults from which we can deduce much about gender presuppositions. This applies particularly to the Magna Mater and Isis cults, which were characterized by all kinds of extrovert behaviour – dancing, cross-dressing, wild hair or shaven heads, self-flagellation and even castration. Cults that encourage such behaviour, such loss of dignity and control, provide a stark contrast to the established Greco-Roman cults whose priesthoods clearly reflected the hierarchical structure of secular society. On this question Richard Gordon makes the astute comment, 'for ecstasy involves the loss of that dignity so carefully projected by the honorific statues which enshrine so much of the civic elite behavioural ideal'.[286] In identifying the oriental cults as essentially within the province of popular culture, Gordon recognized in them a critique of the static strata of Roman society: 'To the extent that the older oriental cults provided specialized institutions for the expression of popular cultural religious goals, they can properly be seen as forms of resistance to dominant elite goals.'[287]

Thus a cult such as Magna Mater provided an 'other' to set against Roman norms of societal and gender definition. Those norms were guarded by legislation. Native Romans, for example, were prohibited from being *galli*: 'by a law and decree of the senate no native Roman walks in procession through the city arrayed in a multi-coloured robe, begging alms or escorted by flute players, or worships the goddess with the Phrygian ceremonies.'[288] Castration was also explicitly forbidden for any Roman of any rank whether free or slave, according to an edict of the Emperor Hadrian. Beard refers to an account by Valerius Maximus, written in the first century CE, according to which a *gallus* named Genucius was deprived of his rights by the Roman judiciary.[289] He had been left a legacy which was appealed against and not granted to him on the grounds that he was neither male nor female and was, therefore, not eligible to inherit under Roman law. Beard notes, 'Genucius was not even allowed to plead his case in public, "for fear that the tribunal of magistrates should be polluted by his obscene presence and corrupt voice".'[290] In line with Gordon's critique of the status of the Magna Mater and Isis cults in Rome, Beard sees the *galli* phenomenon as an alternative within the Roman experience:

> On the one hand was the routinized, formal approach of traditional priesthood, embedded in the political and social hierarchies of the city. On the other hand were the claims of the galli that they enjoyed direct inspiration from the gods – an inspiration that came with frenzy and trance, open to anyone, without consideration of political or social status. . . . By challenging the position of the Roman elite as the sole guardians of access to the gods, the eunuch priests were effectively challenging the wider authority of that elite and the social and cultural norms they have long guaranteed.[291]

Magna Mater, then, could be seen to have been something of a 'Trojan horse' to the Romans, who had at first welcomed her into the heart of their city. Beard argues convincingly, however, that in playing the role of the 'other' in Roman society, the cult of Magna Mater offered a necessary and vital measuring rod by which an identity could be produced for the state. Although Rome might appear to be a classic model of political, social and cultural organisation, as an outcome of its programme of vast expansionism and its exposure to such strong influences as Hellenism, the centre of the Empire might appear, under closer scrutiny, to have been quite shaky after all. Beard observes how scholars have tended to focus on the religious scene on the periphery of the Empire, noting the impact which, for example, the introduction of the 'Emperor Cult' had in such contexts.

Alternatively the ridicule and distaste shown by the Roman reactionaries to the strangeness of foreign cults and customs is understood in terms of racism or xenophobia. To explain these responses in terms of uncertainty and insecurity at the heart of the foundations of Roman society has not been customary among classical scholars. Beard argues:

> There was a necessary and unresolved tension between, on the one hand, a sense of specific identity in the city of Rome, with its language traditions, political inheritance, and religious forms, and on the other, a baffling erosion of that identity as political privileges were shared with the outside, as the literary and artistic traditions of the Greek world came to inform Roman expression, and as Roman religious symbols merged with strange foreign cults and ritual practices. What was it to be Roman in any definable sense, when Rome was synonymous with the world?[292]

Magna Mater functioned on two fronts; first, as an attractive alternative to the traditional Roman cults, offering a liberating change of attitude and order particularly for the 'non-elite', and, second, as an alternative expression of what was not 'Roman'. It performed the role of the 'other' to Roman religion, culture and society, and, implicitly, politics.

Thus the figure of the goddess Magna Mater can be seen as the essential embodiment of 'gynophobia'. The ultimate expression of male devotion to this goddess was self-emasculation. This is the feature that most captured Rome's fearful imagination, and led to the law forbidding any Roman to join the priesthood, and making it almost impossible for any Roman wealth to pass into the possession of its deformed priests. The horror expressed at the *galli* was directed particularly at their continued refusal to pass out of the realms of maleness. Despite possessing castrated bodies, and clad and adorned as women, the *galli* did not wish to cross over in gender terms and join the ranks of women. They were not transsexuals, they remained men, and, as such, a challenge to the norms of maleness.

To some the presence of the Magna Mater cult in the heart of Rome was a constant, undermining threat to Roman patriarchal society. It threatened the norm of gender identity, in its crudest form. A significant number of the Roman elite held that a society in which women have power and authority means anarchy and revolution,[293] and this cult with a goddess at its head was naturally a focus for reactionary sentiment. The evidence needs to be read 'against the grain', as it is by Gordon and others: such foreign cults were most attractive to those who did not possess significant social standing. While being aware that this side of the debate is not so explicitly documented, the fact that the animosity to these cults was so vociferous is evidence in itself for the significant support these cults enjoyed. Although there is no evidence to build a full and detailed picture of the types of people most attracted by Magna Mater and other such 'foreign' cults, the attractions for those without social 'ordo' according to the firmly established strata of Roman society would seem obvious. In such cults, ignoring the niceties of the accepted social norms, priests asked for money rather than offering it, and the conventional customs of dress and etiquette were lampooned by cross-dressing, disordered hair-styles and wild behaviour in the streets. Women in particular would have enjoyed the freedom that such a cult offered them as an alternative to the rigid, patriarchal structures Roman society imposed upon them.

When we set the Magna Mater cult beside the state cults which focused on the Emperor and the imperial household, the extent to which the former posed a challenge to the latter becomes evident. Gordon comments in relation to the sacrificial practice of state religion that: 'it is clear that one of the roles of the *princeps* (the crucial figure at the centre of the sacrifice) as *pontifex maximus* (high priest) was to safeguard the integrity and continuity of the traditional public rituals of Rome.'[294] The public involvement of the Emperor himself as the key figure in these rituals reinforced the structure of Roman social stratification, its political system and its established culture. Gordon argues that the emphasis placed on state religion by the imperial household was an attempt to hold on to the normative centre, and protect it from the pluralism so readily available in the provinces:

> And one of its [imperial religion's] ideological functions in the early Principate was to insulate Rome from the cultural consequences of her own imperialism: the religion of Rome became a guarantee not merely of her supremacy but also of her freedom from contamination by her subjects.... Rome was different from her Empire and her religion was an emblem of that difference.[295]

Such a picture of state cultic religion with the Emperor as chief officiator and all the other priestly offices held by Romans of high social rank, and the ritual of sacrifice itself being a clean and tidy task, highlights the stark contrast between it and the Magna Mater cult.

While for the traditionalists Magna Mater unconsciously helped to articulate what being Roman meant by being precisely what it was not, there were others, certainly not those with any significant investment in Rome's higher social orders, who found that being 'unRoman' could be a liberating and attractive experience. The state cults offered a confirmation of Rome's conscious social stratification, while at the same time those marginalized by this stratification could themselves be confirmed by a religion that exploded it.

The evidence from the Magna Mater cult is crucial for our discussion of gender definition, by providing a vivid example of how given gender categories can be questioned and challenged by religion. If we compare a cult like that of the Emperor with the Magna Mater cult, we find that the prescribed gender roles are inextricably tied to the structure of patriarchal family and society. The male head of the imperial family is the Emperor; he is also head of the state and the Empire. The male role of authority and power is clearly in place, benevolently supporting the imperial cult, and as head of the priests, controlling the life and death of the sacrificial victim. Traditional, prescribed gender roles, confirmed in family as well as political structure, can thus be understood to provide the rigid, strong and unquestioned structure that signified Rome's inner strength at home and the secret of imperial success abroad. Beard and Gordon have demonstrated that both the fear of foreign ideas and cults and their popularity were in part due to the insecurity and loss of identity brought about by the large-scale expansionism that was a feature of this period. Gender identity and the ways in which it may be defined are key illustrations of the inner workings of society. When they are questioned, then society itself is questioned.

While Magna Mater offered an order of priests who transformed and explored the concept of male gender to its extremes, the cult of Vesta could be seen to test the traditional expectations of, and for, female gender in Greco-Roman culture just as extensively, if not as flamboyantly. We noted earlier in our study some of the ways in which the Vestal Virgins transcended the restrictions placed on women in Greco-Roman society.[296] As we saw, they had social and political freedoms normally available only to men, and only to men of high social status. They had a degree of autonomy in respect of their finances, travel and social life. They could be the esteemed instruments of a Senate investigation, as in the case of a man infiltrating the women-only nocturnal ritual of the Bona Dea cult.[297] We must now investigate more closely the notion of female gender represented by this group of women and how it was accommodated in Roman society.

There is no uncertainty or ambivalence regarding the centrality of the Vestal Virgins within traditional Roman life. The cult of Vesta was an integral feature of Roman state religion. They were granted, 'a permanent occupation in guarding the sacred hearth of the city and they lived with their work, fully supported by the state, in a special residence next to the temple of Vesta in the forum'.[298] The distinctive characteristics of the Vestal Virgins have tended to be too readily narrowed down to their virginal chastity, so that other distinctive social markers which they share with matrons and men have sometimes been overlooked. In her essay on the Vestal Virgins Beard draws on Mary Douglas' work to focus on this threefold ambiguity which she classifies as 'interstitial', that is, falling between 'natural' or given categories.[299] This gives us a clue to its sacred and powerful role in Roman society. As we noted earlier, Beard recognizes in the phenomenon of the Vestal Virgins, especially in their given ambiguities, the intention to empower the city of Rome: their unique and vital energies were believed to energize the heart of the Empire. In noting the ambiguity regarding their female gender on the one hand and their status in society on the other, she sees a fusing of the two genders that ignites the city.[300]

While acknowledging the importance of Beard's historical and anthropological approach, a feminist critique of the phenomenon of the Vestal Virgins is a useful analysis alongside Beard's, given the patriarchal structure and functioning of Greco-Roman society. The Vestal Virgins are an example of a male-defined idealized womanhood, which disempowers women according to their nature and empowers them according to male social values. They exist because of male interest and initiative, and any advantage they may have in comparison with other women in that society is a by-product rather than a reason for the institution itself.

They are taken out of society before they are women, as premenstrual girls of 6, and remain sexually inactive on pain of death.[301] As 'de-sexed' women they are then 'safe' to be granted some powers that only men, the first gender in Roman society, can properly expect to exercise. They can enjoy a close relationship with the institution of the Senate and socialize as individuals with the most influential people of the day. The Emperor as high priest ensured that their social status was the highest attainable for any woman, save the Emperor's immediate family, and even they, as women, lacked the many freedoms granted the Vestal Virgins.

The privileged ground they occupied took them outside the

boundaries of female experience. Their manifestation of a unique understanding of what it was to be women separated them from other women. As 'matrons' they were relatively more free than other unmarried, childless women, as 'men' they were, in certain strictly ordained and controlled categories, the most liberated women in acceptable society. Ultimately, men remained in control of these women, which is most clearly illustrated in the account of the horrible and fatal retribution which awaited any Vestal Virgin who might venture beyond permitted behaviour and engage in sexual relations.[302]

In this critique, the explanation for the existence and centrality of the Vestal Virgins within Roman state religion can be understood as male appropriation of female powers of regeneration to channel them for the regeneration of Rome and the Empire. The sexual energy of the Vestal Virgins, imaged by the continual fire burning in the temple, could ignite Rome to a glorious future and endless victories. These women were deliberately taken out of normal society while their fertility was at its height. They would have been initiated, between the ages of 6 and 10, before menstruation began, and stay within the priesthood for a minimum of thirty years, that is, for the most fertile span of a woman's life. Female energy was thus being reined in by patriarchy to be redirected towards the achievement of military power and political supremacy.

We have taken two examples from Greco-Roman religion to examine the role religion might have played in the construction or confirmation of gender. If we can represent religious experience within the Roman Empire as a spectrum with state religion at one end and non-Roman religions at the other, then our two examples are deliberately chosen from each of the contrasting extremes. The cult of Vesta, with its physical presence so close to the imperial household, and with an Emperor as its high priest, is the ultimate religious expression of the state itself. The Magna Mater cult, although welcomed into the heart of the city of Rome, stands in stark contrast as a religious experience coming in from 'outside', and with its practices that, simply by their existence, questioned the accepted norms of Roman society.

These contrasting religious expressions lead to some interesting conclusions for our discussion of gender roles. The Vesta cult with its group of sanctified virgins confirms the essentialist view of female gender, that is to say, there is a natural role for both sexes, determined by biological differences and reflected in and supported by tra-

128

ditional society. In other words reproduction is the function that prescribes the status and role of women. This is the view that lies at the heart of the phenomenon of the Vestal Virgins in ancient Rome. Their overriding feature is their sexuality. I agree with Beard that their virginal status was not the only significant feature that marked them out as 'holy' from the rest of society,[303] but it is the primary feature in the sense that it was for disobedience in sexual matters that they could be put to death. The Virgins were recognized through the harnessing of what was believed to be their essential female nature.

The *galli* of the Magna Mater cult, by contrast, reveal the extensive nature of society's gender construction. By actualizing alternatives to prescribed and accepted gender roles, this group threatened to undermine the self-confidence of the imperial state. Being men in their own minds, despite displaying signals of female identity, and even removing the biological mark of masculinity, the *galli* displayed how far sexual identity is a matter of construction in the eyes of society: a society that cannot accept them as male. Where the Vestal Virgins supported and reinforced the hierarchical and patriarchal structure of Roman society, the cult of Magna Mater with its *galli* priests demonstrated the deconstruction of that society. They had a priesthood that begged alms *from* society rather than demonstrated its wealth and power *to* society, and that celebrated its sacrifices with an anarchic display of blood rather than a demonstration of control over the flow of life.

The contrast is further reflected in the adherents of the two; the cult of Vesta was for those who had much invested in society as it was, while the cult of Magna Mater offered an alternative for those who were marginalized by the rigid social structures, and could only gain from change.

8

WISDOM, LILITH
AND MOTHERS

We have noted previously the essentially patriarchal nature of
Judaism in socio-religious terms, and we have also observed that in
an environment within a society where female participation is visible,
Judaism adapts. Following the work of Bernadette Brooten, we
considered the evidence for women leaders of synagogues and
women elders within Jewish communities in the Diaspora.[304] In
relation to this period we discussed also the *Book of Judith* in which a
woman is the central character who saves her people by ingenuity
and strength in the face of an awesome enemy. We noted that this
ambivalence is affirmed by the evidence of the Mishnah, the earliest
collection of rabbinic Jewish teaching, where, in line with the study
made by Judith Wegner, women appear as both 'chattel' and
'person'.[305] In attempting to account for this ambivalence we stressed
the changing political and cultural contexts confronted by Judaism
during the period of the late Republic and early Empire. Hellenistic
culture and values had a particularly significant part to play in
confirming a subordinate role for women in society.

Many of the Jewish literary sources written in the Greek language,
from the second century BCE to the first century CE, contain a clear
inclination not only towards holding women in a position of
subservience, but also expressing a misogynist attitude. Women are
not simply the second sex constantly affirming the primacy of the
first, but they are the 'other' gender which actually manifests evil in
the world, and ensnares men, dragging them down to ruin and
despair. Women are represented as a power against good, the latter
being the natural inclination for men.

Within Jewish literature this tendency, in its least sinister form,
first appears in the Hebrew wisdom tradition,[306] and only later
intensifies in the Greek form of that tradition. The Book of Proverbs

130

contains advice for those who want to be successful in worldly terms, that is, to have wealth and influence in the highest circles. In the wisdom tradition aspirations like these meet with divine blessing. Advice to men concerning their dealings with women includes the comment that, while an encounter with a prostitute is merely the cost of a loaf of bread, to sleep with another man's wife could well cost a man his life (Prov. 6.26). The very concept of true wisdom is poetically depicted as a 'good' woman in this literary genre.[307] In the following passage Wisdom[308] builds her house and invites men to dine with her and imbibe truth and knowledge:

> Wisdom has built her house,
> she has hewn her seven pillars.
> She has slaughtered her animals,
> she has mixed her wine,
> she has set her table.
> She has sent out her servant girls,
> she calls from the highest places in the town,
> 'You that are simple, turn in here!'
> To those without sense she says, 'Come, eat of my bread and
> drink the wine I have mixed.
> Lay aside immaturity, and live,
> and walk in the way of insight.'
>
> Prov. 9.1–6

In this passage Wisdom stands in contrast to the loud and foolish woman who epitomizes ignorance: the invitation to her house is an invitation to Sheol, the place of the dead (Prov. 9.13–18). In an earlier passage the rich gains to be made by adhering to the path of wisdom are underlined again by contrasting it with the fatal error of being seduced by an adulterous woman (7.4–23). Wisdom offers life and true wealth:

> 'Hear, for I will speak noble things,
> and from my lips will come what is right;
> for my mouth will utter truth;
> wickedness is an abomination to my lips . . .
> Take instruction instead of silver,
> and knowledge rather than choice gold;
> for wisdom is better than jewels,
> and all that you may desire cannot compare with her.'
>
> Prov. 8.6–7, 10–11

Wisdom's words are given credibility by asserting her divine power: 'By me kings reign, and rulers decree what is just; by me rulers rule, and nobles, all who govern rightly' (Prov. 8.15–16). Her status is affirmed through her pre-eminence in God's creation: she traces her origin progressively further back to the very moment when the primeval waters became subject to divine creative energy:

> The Lord created me at the beginning of his work,
> the first of his acts of long ago.
> Ages ago I was set up, at the first,
> before the beginning of the earth.
> When there were no depths I was brought forth,
> when there were no springs abounding with water.
> Before the mountains had been shaped,
> before the hills, I was brought forth –
> when he had not yet made earth and fields,
> or the world's first bits of soil.
> When he established the heavens, I was there,
> when he drew a circle on the face of the deep,
> when he made firm the skies above,
> when he established the fountains of the deep.
>
> Prov. 8.22–28

At this stage in the wisdom tradition women are used to personify both the right way and the wrong way for a man to live his life. There is no significant indication of misogyny, merely a typical reflection of patriarchal society where men's decisions concerning how they conduct themselves are of primary importance. Women are set within the domestic sphere, and their presence is there to serve and support male interests. The inclination, however, to identify the 'good' woman with concepts beyond human experience, as in the passage quoted above where she is a witness to creation itself, and to identify the 'bad' woman with the more concrete experience of adultery is evident.

It is this inclination that intensifies and eventually materializes as misogyny in later Jewish literature. This tendency was no doubt encouraged by the influence of Hellenistic thought of the type found in Aristotle's work.[309] When we turn to another text belonging to the same genre as Proverbs but displaying more obvious Hellenistic influence, we can illustrate this intensification. The *Wisdom of Jesus ben Sirach*, an apocryphal work commonly referred to as *Sirach*,

132

continues the tradition of the female personification of the concept of wisdom, and in the same idealistic terms:

Wisdom teaches her children
and gives help to those who seek her.
Whoever loves her loves life,
and those who seek her from early morning are filled with joy.
Whoever holds her fast inherits glory,
and the Lord blesses the place she enters.
Those who serve her minister to the Holy One;
the Lord loves those who love her.

4.11–14

Wisdom's unique pre-existent relationship with God is maintained: 'Before the ages, in the beginning, he created me, and for all the ages I shall not cease to be' (Sir. 24.9). Also, the contrast between the woman Wisdom and the adulterous women found in Proverbs is clearly discernible too.[310] In the passage immediately preceding the hymn in praise of Wisdom (Sir. 24), we find a diatribe aimed at the woman who would deceive her husband. It is part of a sustained warning against 'sins of the flesh' which has already dealt with incestuous fornication and unfaithful husbands, before addressing the wife who plays the harlot:

So it is with the woman who leaves her husband and presents him with an heir by another man. For first of all she has disobeyed the law of the Most High; second, she has committed an offence against her husband; and third, through her fornication she has committed adultery and brought forth children by another man.

(23.22–23)

The account of this woman is set immediately before we encounter the perfect woman, Wisdom, who enjoys the divine presence, and exists as a force for good when sent into the world. Immediately following the hymn to Wisdom is advice on creating harmony in the home and in life generally, written from a male perspective and culminating in an emotional attack on 'wicked women':

There is no venom worse than a snake's venom, and no anger worse than a woman's wrath. I would rather live with a lion and a dragon than live with an evil woman. A woman's wickedness changes her appearance, and darkens her face like

133

that of a bear. Her husband sits among the neighbors, and he cannot help sighing bitterly. Any iniquity is small compared to a woman's iniquity; may a sinner's lot befall her! A sandy ascent for the feet of the aged – such is a garrulous wife to a quiet husband.

(25.15–20)

This is followed by a warning to men against living in a relationship where the woman is the main provider, a situation about which, as we saw in relation to the situation in ancient Sparta, Aristotle was particularly concerned.[311]

A particularly sinister dimension enters the text when the writer justifies the intensity of his warning against women by reference to scripture: 'From a woman sin had its beginning, and because of her we all die' (25.24). The very existence of sin in the world is attributed to the action of one woman, which has had fatal repercussions for all subsequent humanity. The writer is drawing on biblical creation mythology, where the first couple, Adam and Eve, were offered an alternative to obeying the words of their creator by a serpent (Gen. 3). The woman took the initiative, ate the forbidden fruit, and shared it with the man. Christian theology, more so than Jewish, has been fixated with the issue of the culpability aspect to this myth, a myth traditionally believed to be an accurate account not only of how the world was created, but also of the nature of the relationships between the divine and humanity, and between men and women. Some of the most influential Christian theologians, including Augustine, Ambrose and Aquinas, have focused on the woman as the individual with particular responsibility for the act of disobedience. Her action of offering the fruit to the man is seen to be the moment when sin entered the world: the moment when lust was ignited in the man by the woman was the moment when sin was first manifested in the world.

Judaism and Christianity provide various ways of understanding how sin went beyond the immediate experience of the first couple. Frequently within Christian theology, formulated most clearly by Augustine, we find sin explained as though it were some type of genetic disease. From the moment it was manifested through the action of Eve, sin became part of the human make-up, and inescapable since it was injected into each individual whenever sexual relations occurred in the process of procreation. Sin and sex become inextricably linked together in this type of Christian theology. The doctrine of original sin emerged and the created world was understood in essentially pessimistic terms with the human race a fallen race, and the earth itself the habitat for sinful life.

This is one result of what can happen when so much emphasis is placed on the implications of the first couple's act of disobedience. In the context of Jewish theology we are offered alternative explanations which stem from a somewhat different understanding of human nature.[312] There are many examples in Jewish literature where the idea is expressed that the effect of Adam and Eve's action was not to infect the nature of all subsequent humanity so that no individual could ever be born without sin (apart from those born from immaculate conceptions). Rather, instead of believing that individuals are alienated from God because of inherent sinful natures, Jewish theology suggests that the overwhelming presence of sin in the world is the result of humanity following Adam and Eve's example. Each person possesses the ability to choose between good and evil, because each person is born with a good inclination (*yetser ha-tov*) and a bad inclination (*yetser ha-ra*) in equal measure. The bad inclination tends to dominate, however, since the actions of that inclination are the most evident in the world and have been since the time of Adam and Eve.[313] One good illustration from our period comes from the apocryphal *Book of Baruch*: 'Adam is therefore not the cause, save only of his own soul, but each of us has been the Adam of his own soul' (2 Baruch 54.19).

The comment in *Sirach* with which we began this part of our discussion concerning the unique link that exists between women and sin, becomes more evident and more offensive when Christianity expresses its theology concerning the origin of sin in the fourth and fifth centuries CE. Such later reflection should not be read into a comment made in a text written some five or six centuries earlier. But what we might suggest is that later Christian theology shows the possible logical extremes such an idea can be taken to when it is developed in a context of virulent misogyny. In its second-century BCE context in *Sirach* the identification of women with sin is only one view reflecting one part of Jewish Hellenistic thought: such an isolated comment should not be taken as normative for the wide spectrum of Jewish belief and practice during our period.

We can discern in the wisdom tradition, however, even in early examples like *Sirach*, a tendency to understand sexual transgressions, that is to say, acts of fornication or adultery that upset the institution of the family, as the result of women's provocation. *Sirach*, in commenting on the trouble a headstrong daughter can cause to a family, deliberately chooses shocking language and obscene imagery: 'As a thirsty traveller opens his mouth and drinks from any water near him, so she will sit in front of every tent peg and open her quiver to the arrow' (26.12). This tendency is made explicit when the same writer cites a proverb elsewhere: 'Better is the wickedness of a man than a woman who does good; it is a woman who brings shame and disgrace' (42.14).

In his discussion of the conflicting images of women in the Jewish sources of the Greco-Roman period,[314] Pieter van der Horst observes that the misogyny found in *Sirach* is a tendency that recurs, for example, in the work of the first-century CE Jewish philosopher Philo of Alexandria and his younger contemporary, the Jewish historian Josephus. He points to Philo's advice to keep wives as one would keep slaves,[315] and Josephus' comment that Adam was punished by God because he yielded to a woman's counsel.[316] The influence of a particular strand of Hellenistic and in particular Aristotelian thought on these writers, including the author of *Sirach*, is undeniable. But as van der Horst comments, these texts reflect only one attitude to women, and this should not be understood as normative to Judaism, whose traditions were as pluralistic on the question of gender as those of Hellenism generally and early Christianity:

> It is clear that in early Judaism a monolithic and exclusively negative image of women never had a monopoly position. In this respect ancient Judaism was not essentially different from contemporary Christianity or Hellenism.[317]

These examples from the wisdom tradition and later Hellenistic Jewish texts, show how the fusion of Judaism and Hellenism that took place before and during our period could produce a particularly virulent type of misogyny stemming from an essentialist understanding of gender. Once philosophers and religious thinkers are persuaded that gender is an essential aspect of an individual's nature, in biological and psychological terms, it follows that gender might dictate particular character traits, peculiar only to that gender. In the examples we have looked at, most obvious in *Sirach*, the female gender is depicted as displaying behaviour which reflects the 'natural' female inclination to trick and seduce.

Other examples describe a 'natural' inclination to serve. The author of *Sirach* sets his opinions concerning female gender in a religious context, pleading with God to spare him the fate of encountering the entrapment of women, describing a 'wicked' woman as a curse, and a 'good' woman as a blessing. The woman Wisdom is set in contrast to the woman who follows her natural inclination, but, unlike the 'harlot' or 'adulteress', Wisdom cannot really be identified with real women. No real woman, for example, would claim to have existed beside the divinity while the world was being created. Despite her lofty status at the right hand of the divine, even Wisdom herself experiences existence as the 'second' sex. Her role is essentially a passive one, realizing the aspirations of the proactive God. She is 'given' to people and becomes a source for God's will to be realized in the world. She calls to men in the streets and invites them into her sphere, the domestic home.

During the Hellenistic period, the notion of Torah, the divine law, develops in Judaism to become a divine attribute often identified with wisdom, indeed often replacing the concept of wisdom. This is quite logical: the Torah is understood as the unique revelation of the divine will, so its identification with divine wisdom follows as a consequence. In *Sirach*, which reflects an early stage in this development, Wisdom invites Israel to eat of her fruits, which she identifies with the fruits of studying the Torah: 'all this is the book of the covenant of the Most High God, the law that Moses commanded us as an inheritance for the congregations of Jacob' (24.23). In later texts Torah, a feminine noun like wisdom (Hebrew *hokmah*), is also 'given' to Israel. Again, the concept, personified as a woman, is granted only a passive role, illustrated in later midrash by being described as a daughter of the divine, given by her father to the bridegroom chosen for her, Moses.[318] Even the most idealized notion of female gender within this extensive strand of Jewish thought ultimately reflects a passive role. Action remains in the male arena of the god Yahweh and his human representative Moses.

This provides theological underpinning for another philosophical notion concerning the relationship between nature and gender. In an earlier chapter we could observe a more constructionist view of gender in operation in a Jewish context, in the case of female Jewish elders and leaders of synagogues, where influence, sound judgement and wealth were the key factors, not preconditioned notions of what was prescribed behaviour for men or women. In that context being female could mean many things within a very broad spectrum of possibilities for both men and women, not a narrow definition based on an essentialist understanding of women as the second sex, with very limited expectations in the public realm. Examples of women functioning effectively in the public realm in the ancient world are manifestations of an alternative understanding of gender.

Judaism, as has been noted more than once, does display an ambivalence in regard to women's nature, character and status. Although often appearing overtly patriarchal, the pluralistic phenomenon that was ancient Jewish society and culture, as we have shown, meant that a monolithic and essentialist view of female gender as an estimation of its belief and practice is not viable. As an illustration of this understanding of ancient Judaism the mythic figure of Lilith has become a focus for contemporary Jewish feminism, particularly that which attempts to reclaim the past in an attempt to reform the present.[319]

Lilith only appears once in biblical literature, and even that appearance is denied her by some translators who have 'screech-owl', 'night hag', 'night-jar' or the like for the Hebrew word *lilith* in Isaiah 34.14.[320] The Catholic *Jerusalem Bible* and the ecumenical *New Revised Standard Version* both translate it as a proper name 'Lilith'. The context is one of divine wrath and vengeance and the whole chapter is an extended image of anarchic devastation:

> They shall call it No Kingdom There, and its princes shall be nothing. Thorns shall grow over its strongholds, nettles and thistles in its fortresses. It shall be the haunt of jackals, an abode for ostriches. Wildcats shall meet with hyenas, goat-demons shall call to each other; there too Lilith shall repose, and find a place to rest.
>
> (34.12–14)

This enigmatic reference gave scriptural authority for a popular belief, and fuelled the imagination of commentators who asked themselves: who is this creature, what was her origin and purpose?[321] Her name echoed the Hebrew word for night, *lailah*, which led to her identification with those universal primeval fears of darkness.[322] She became the 'bogey-woman' of popular superstition and was associated in particular with nocturnal visits to homes to kill or sicken children. A tradition quoted in the collection of midrashic material known as the *Alphabet of Ben Sira* attempts to explain the origin of the fears associated with Lilith. A recent article by Barbara Borts attempts to read the Lilith tradition 'against the grain' and reclaim her as a source of empowerment for women seeking equality within Judaism today. She includes a useful translation of the relevant passage from the usually inaccessible text of the *Alphabet of Ben Sira*.

The passage begins with the creation of woman, a creation prompted by Adam's need for a companion, but the outcome was not what either God or Adam intended:

> When the Holy One, Blessed be He, created the first Adam as a solitary creature, God said, 'It is not good for Adam to be alone.' God created woman from the earth like him and called her Lilith. Suddenly they began competing/arguing with each other. Said she, 'I will not lie underneath', and he said, 'I will not lie underneath, but rather on top, for you were designated to be on the bottom and I on the top.' She said to him, 'The two of us are equal as we were both created from the earth.'[323]

Lilith sees the impossibility of the union, blasphemously utters the divine name and absconds. Adam reports the situation to God who despatches three angels to search for Lilith with the ultimatum that, if she does not return, she will witness the death of a hundred of her children every day. She is eventually caught by the angels but retorts to the ultimatum with violent threats of the same order, promising to be the bringer of sickness to children. To free herself from the angels' attempts to destroy her, she promises them that she will not strike a child in a place where she sees their names inscribed on an amulet.

The key feature of the Lilith tradition that attracts the attention of modern feminist commentators is her relationship with Adam, and the subsequent decision to create another woman, Eve, deliberately different in temperament from the first. This tradition reflects a concept of equality which originally existed between the sexes in Jewish thought, even if it was subsequently 'corrected' by the creation of Eve in line with notions of 'first' and 'second' sex. No doubt within the context of Jewish midrash the Lilith tradition, with its dire portrayal of a woman who would seek equality, functions as an illustration of sexual hierarchy. But the fact that such a tradition exists at all can be interpreted to mean that the notion of equality was an issue within ancient Judaism.

Certain evidence collected and interpreted by Brooten,[324] would allow us to take this argument even a step further and argue that such an egalitarian understanding of women's status was actually practised in some forms of Judaism in the Diaspora. Literary evidence from alternative strands of Judaism discussed previously[325] gives further support to this argument. Before drawing our discussion of

Jewish notions of female gender to a conclusion, we need to glance at another strand of Jewish tradition which provides important insights into the question of the role religion plays in the construction of male gender.

The Israelite 'fathers', Abraham, Isaac and Jacob, and 'mothers', Sarah, Rebecca, Rachel and Leah, are perhaps the most familiar biblical characters since they play a central role in the literary heritage of Christians and Muslims as well as Jews. The naming of these figures as 'patriarchs' and 'matriarchs' is important to our present discussion because these individuals are 'founding' figures, prescribing expectations and experiences for men and women. From the outset a discrepancy is apparent between the two groups: there are three patriarchs and four matriarchs. The patriarchal nature of biblical Israelite society is evident in that one of the men, Jacob, has two wives, Rachel and Leah. This imbalance between patriarchs and matriarchs is compounded when we discover that Abraham also is a husband of more than one woman, and that, since one woman, Hagar, does not serve the interests of the nation through the offspring she bears, she is not esteemed in Jewish biblical terms as a 'matriarch' at all.

By referring to these groups of men and women in parallel categories, patriarchs and matriarchs, one might imagine that they correspond with one another, not only in biblical tradition but in subsequent commentaries and religious literature. When we examine the attributes that are upheld for each group, however, we discover that this is not the case. It might be argued that they are complementary rather than parallel or identical in the interests of their partnerships, but a complementary relationship has to be extremely well balanced to avoid falling into a hierarchical one, where one plays the supportive role to the main character.

According to the biblical narrative, Abraham and Sarah, as a couple, have been unable to have children. They are now 99 and 90 years old respectively, and so their hopes for bearing offspring together had long been dashed. When the narrative that recounts the miracle of a child being born to them begins, what is immediately striking is the indirect nature of the intended mother's encounter with the divine:

> And God said to Abraham, 'As for Sarah your wife, you shall not call her name Sarai, but Sarah shall be her name. I will bless her, and moreover I will give you a son by her. I will bless her

and she shall give rise to nations; kings of peoples shall come
from her.'

(Gen. 17.15–16)

Commenting on this passage from the standpoint of feminist critique, Esther Fuchs notes that throughout Sarah remains the silent
partner: she is not even allowed to be present on the occasion of the
annunciation of the birth of her son Isaac. She is talked about, not
to: 'Yahweh blesses Sarah in her absence and changes her name
through her husband.'[326] Fuchs also notes that it is Abraham and not
Sarah who is the true recipient of the promised son, since the son is
to be born to and for Abraham by Sarah. Sarah's status is that of the
means of reproduction, the instrument through whom God will keep
his promise to Abraham. So in the story concerning the miraculous
birth of Isaac to the hitherto barren Sarah, it is the patriarch Abraham
who is the central character and it is to him that God's promises are
made, not to Sarah the matriarch.

Sarah cannot be seen as having an intimate relationship with God
in any way comparable to that of her husband or the other patriarchs.
Even when the news of Isaac's promised birth is repeated (Gen.
18.9ff.), and Sarah is present, she is only allowed to eavesdrop on the
conversation, not participate in it. In overhearing the news that she
is to bear a son, it is hardly surprising that she laughs: as a 90-year-
old it is a ludicrous suggestion, even when the suggestion comes from
God. But this reaction is used as a measuring rod beside Abraham's
notorious faith in God's promises. Abraham left his home on the
promise of a better land (Gen. 12). He did not laugh at the idea that
an aged couple would produce a child.

Sarah's main claim to fame in the biblical tradition lies in the belief
that she is biologically the 'mother' of Israel, that is, the female
ancestor of God's elect. It is her ability, or at one time her inability,
to bear children that singles Sarah out for attention. Her ultimate
justification comes from bearing a child, a male child: she thus fulfils
the necessary requirement for biblical women.[327]

According to the Bible, even the relationship she has with that
child, with Isaac, is restricted. For example, as soon as Isaac is born
he is taken away by Abraham and named and circumcised. When we
are told of God's plan to kill her only son (Gen. 22), the text allows
no insight into Sarah's emotions at that time. The importance of her
motherhood ends with the production of the baby. This is not true
of Jewish post-biblical tradition relating to this part of the story. The

midrash attempts to answer some of the questions raised by the text by giving an account of Sarah's feelings and actions at that time. For example, by taking seriously the point that in the biblical text Sarah's death is recorded immediately after Abraham's attempt to sacrifice Isaac at God's command, her death is interpreted as the direct result of her shock on hearing of Abraham's action.[328] According to Jewish tradition, even Sarah's ultimate fate is the result of a conspiracy between God and Abraham to deprive her of her beloved son, whose own near fate becomes Sarah's own.

Set in the midst of the story of Isaac's birth is the story of Abraham and Sarah and the Pharaoh of Egypt (Gen. 12.10ff.). Sarah plays an important part in this, and acts as a character independent of her motherhood, but she is hardly represented as acting on her own behalf. Abraham passes her off as his sister and gives her to the Pharaoh, and it is only through the intervention of God that she is saved from being forced to commit an adulterous act. Again Sarah can be seen as simply the passive victim of a patriarchal society with its patriarchal God.

We can see the same type of treatment applied to the other mothers of Israel. Rachel Adler argues for a more positive role for the four matriarchs.[329] She admits that their role is primarily one of nurturing, particularly in cases where the fertility of the women is taken out of their hands and put in God's control. But she sees their action as being politically powerful, even ruthless on behalf of their favourite sons, as, for example, in the stories of Sarah's casting out of Hagar (Gen. 21), and Rebecca's hoodwinking of her husband in order to dispossess Esau (Gen. 27).

A recent study by Danna Fewell and David Gunn underlines this observation and notes it as a central theme running through biblical narrative in its presentation of key female characters.[330] In the case of women like the matriarchs it is not that they are ignored or given no space in the text: rather what is significant is the manner in which they are presented. Fewell and Gunn take the characterization of the first woman, Eve, in Genesis 3 and observe how her character becomes normative for subsequent key female characters, including the matriarchs. Eve, they conclude, acts despite the social construction that is set out in the story of creation, as much a story of the creation of society as of the material world. From the outset, through the character of Eve, social constructs are challenged so that outcomes are not always those that are expected. This is indicative of the role other female characters will play in the narratives that follow. Sarah ensures that she will be the mother of a nation through the birth of her son, despite the fact that Abraham's other wife, Hagar, has borne him a son before hers (Gen. 21). Rebecca ensures that her favourite son Jacob is his father's heir, in spite of the fact that society would have favoured the first-born Esau (Gen. 27). These women are both powerless according to the constraints of their society and powerful through their manipulation of it. Fewell and Gunn see the character of Eve as foundational for this behaviour and observe her actions being echoed consistently through the narratives:

> Though Eve's behaviour is condemned by God and berated by centuries of readers, she emerges as a character with initiative and courage. Too innocent to be evil, too guileless to be seductive, she is a child testing her boundaries, weighing her options, making her choices. She makes her decision independently of those who claim authority over her. From time to time, in the larger story that follows, we will glimpse Eve's daughters following in her footsteps. They will show initiative, courage, and independence despite societal constraints. Yet just as Eve is eventually cast into the shadow of Adam, not to speak of the tree, women in Genesis–Kings will often shade into invisibility.[331]

In her analysis, Adler, however, cannot ignore the fact that these women are only allowed to be politically astute within the confines of the domestic role of mother. As mothers, they were servants to the higher cause of producing babies who would grow into patriarchal figures like their fathers, sons who would not be passive victims like their mothers, making the best of their circumstances. The text presents the major aim and achievement of these women to be that of producing male children through the intervention of God. This in itself is not meritorious, since biologically women are designed to give birth. Furthermore, it was God who was the enabler of their fertility. Adler notes how effectively in the case of these women both the Bible and Jewish tradition remove all creative activity from the mother, and give it to God:

> The barren woman is useful because she proves God's fertility, so to speak. Hence midrashim from the talmudic to the late medieval collections industrially multiply the number of barren women in the Bible and dramatize the miracle of their conception. According to a Talmudic midrash (b. Yebamoth 64b),

Sarah has no womb. Numbers Rabbah explains that the angel who appeared to Samson's mother was careful to inform her that it was she and not her husband who was the barren one (Naso 10.5). According to Resh Lakish in Ruth Rabbah 6.2, Ruth was forty years old when she became pregnant and had Obed as a miracle. In Ruth Rabbah 7.14, moreover, he asserts that Ruth, too, lacked the main portion of her womb.[332]

The tendency in Jewish tradition was to recognize the passivity of these women in relation to their child-bearing and then to reinforce it. The 'mothers of Israel', we may conclude, are in no way on a par with the 'fathers of Israel'. The matriarchs of biblical and Jewish tradition are esteemed because of their action and initiative as wives and mothers. The patriarchs by contrast are not esteemed, or even referred to in passing, as being self-sacrificing, intelligent husbands and fathers. On the contrary, in the case of Abraham his treatment of both Sarah and Hagar, and most disturbingly his unquestioning, or blind, obedience to the divine command that led him to attempt to murder his young son could never be regarded as a paradigm for perfect family life.

The accounts of the patriarchs and matriarchs, although allowing for interesting and multi-dimensional female characters, are, nevertheless, the products of an essentialist concept of gender construction. The behaviour and values of these men and women are governed by given norms for male and female lives based on their biological functions. Obviously, this observation applies more explicitly to the female characters than to the male. Implicitly, the text does not demand of these men anything more than a brief contribution to the process of procreation: because of their biological make-up, the act of fatherhood is only a small part of their personhood as patriarchs. 'Patriarch', then, is a category that includes something more than fatherhood, a special, direct relationship with God is perhaps its most significant feature, alongside decision making and leadership: merits that exist apart from the domestic sphere. Matriarchs do not go beyond the domestic boundaries, and their influence is always indirect, ensuring their own individual security by ensuring that the sons who cherish them the most become the inheritors of their father's power.

We have chosen three distinct reflections on gender from Jewish tradition: Wisdom, a divine attribute articulated in poetry and personified as a woman; Lilith, a mythological figure; and the matriarchs, essentially literary characters. Of the three, only the Lilith tradition provides an opening to question essentialist notions of gender. In Lilith and Eve two types of womanhood are offered: the former is realized in terms of equality with her male counterpart; the latter in terms of subservience. That these two alternatives can exist side by side in this context suggests that gender is a social construct rather than biologically determined. Lilith is just as female in her challenge to Adam as Eve is in her submission to him.

9

SISTERS IN CHRIST OR DAUGHTERS OF EVE?

When we set Christianity beside Greco-Roman religion and Judaism, it does seem distinct in its explicit attempts to define the nature of women in relation to men. What we discover as implicit in the other traditions is clearly articulated by Christian writers from the first century onwards. Earlier in our discussion of the role of women within the early Christian communities, we noted a diversity of practice that reflected alternative notions of organization and structure.[333] It is this diversity that prompts Christianity's explicit definition of gender, particularly in relation to the nature and role of women. Because there is diversity in terms of women's self-understanding and experience, when Christianity does consciously realize the need to conform to, rather than to challenge, society, it is compelled to argue for a particular understanding of gender. This early development formed the basis for subsequent Christian beliefs about the essential nature of women and men, and the prescriptions regarding the roles each has to fulfil within church and society. The charismatic communities of the first half-century provide the antithesis to the Christian concept of womanhood that emerged by the end of the century.

Within the context of the charismatic communities that were characteristic of the Jesus movement and the early Pauline foundations, gender roles were constructionist rather than essentialist. Men and women could work side by side, preaching and spreading their beliefs about Jesus of Nazareth. Women could opt out of the domestic sphere and enter the public world; they could exist apart from their fathers, husbands or children. The order of 'widows' was a means of realizing this option.[334] By taking on the dress of a widow, a woman gained the ability to move freely within the public sphere, protected from sexual harassment or assault. The guise of widowhood was a means of bypassing the norms of patriarchy, and allowing for an alternative form of existence for women.

This phenomenon within early Christianity begs comparison with the Jewish Therapeutrides of Egypt described by Philo,[335] and, perhaps, the order of Vestal Virgins.[336] All three groups prescribe roles for women that are in stark contrast to the usual expectations of the patriarchal societies to which they belong. In the case of the Vestal Virgins their role is one deliberately constructed by the power-group of their society. Their relative freedoms, which at times place them on a par with men, are granted to them by men. They are a controlled incongruity, as opposed to a challenge to society's norm. The Therapeutrides, along with their male counterpart community of Therapeutae, were a group that withdrew from society. As women who turned their backs on marriage in preference for wisdom 'as a life partner',[337] the Therapeutrides did not seek a role in wider society, rather an option to be apart from it, living in their own society.

In comparison to the Vestal Virgins and the Therapeutrides, the 'widows' of early Christianity, the women co-workers that St Paul mentions in his letters, strike a chord of dissonance within their society. They are not a category that society has formalized, nor are they prepared to withdraw and constitute a community apart. They were women who wished to exercise the same freedoms that men enjoyed in the public sphere, so that they could preach the gospel in which they fervently believed as effectively as the men, if not more so. The impetus for their non-conformity seems to lie within their own psyche. They were convinced that their inward self had been transformed by the death and resurrection of Jesus of Nazareth. Such a belief is well attested in the Pauline letters which constitute the earliest extant evidence we possess of Christianity, and it had profound implications for the understanding of gender roles within the early Christian communities. We noted earlier the baptismal formula in Galatians, for example, which reflected the belief that all social, racial and gender boundaries are dissolved in the community of Christ.[338] At baptism the new believer puts to death the 'old' self, and rises out of the water a new creation:[339]

> Do not lie to one another, seeing that you have stripped off the old self with its practices and have clothed yourselves with the new self, which is being renewed in knowledge according to the image of its creator. In that renewal there is no longer Greek

and Jew, circumcised and uncircumcised, barbarian, Scythian, slave and free; but Christ is all and in all.

(Col. 3.9–11)

This concept of a transformation of the self in early Christianity allowed women to cross boundaries and challenge their identity in radical terms. Being a woman could be redefined in this new context in such a way as to make possible for her a self-understanding and experience that had previously been exclusive to men.

A tension necessarily arose between experience within this new believing community and life outside it where the 'old' norms and expectations for women prevailed. The order of widows is testimony to the compromise that had to exist between the old and the new. If women were to live the new life, spread the gospel and support the embryonic communities in the public sphere, they still had to observe the restrictions society placed on their freedom. They therefore had to present themselves publicly as non-sexual beings, that is, as widows who enjoyed society's protection from men's sexual advances. They did not constitute a group of women who could function in public without their sexuality being their most significant feature. Rather, they were a group who had to 'suspend' their sexuality in order to function freely outside their normative domestic sphere.

The inclusion of women in the earliest phases of Christianity is a feature that is not universal, and to present it as a 'golden age' for women's participation does not represent fully the divergent nature of Christian practice. In contexts where non-conformity to the wider society could have resulted in scapegoating and persecution, the compulsion to reflect rather than to challenge society's structures can easily be understood. The first major persecution of Christians began in 65 CE, instigated by the Emperor Nero who made them responsible for the fire of Rome, but even before this particular incident, sporadic outbreaks of disorder had met with the Empire's heavy fist.[340] In such contexts other structures were appearing, parallel to the charismatic communities we have been considering, and they mirrored the norms of society in terms of organization as well as gender roles.[341]

There was another factor in this too. The beliefs that underpinned women's inclusion in the charismatic communities were bound up with convictions about the imminent return of Christ and the eschatological overturning of earthly authority and power structures.[342] Once those convictions weakened, and Christian beliefs focused on the role of the church in this world rather than the next, the practice of conformity within society had to outweigh any tendency to challenge from without. Women's roles then had to be articulated clearly in the light of divergent practices which did reflect a challenge to, and therefore a criticism of, the endemic patriarchal society.

In order to prescribe modes of behaviour for men and women that reflected rather than challenged the norms of Greco-Roman society, Christianity had to provide the theology that would support its teaching. To be convincing, this theology had to demonstrate that these roles had been part of divine revelation since the time the world was created, or to put it another way, that in God's mind there could be no alternative.

Christianity shared with Judaism the account of Adam and Eve as the primal couple, made by the hand of God to enjoy the fruits of divine creation. The story recounts how the couple quickly demonstrated their independence from God by eating fruit from a tree that had been expressly forbidden to them. Although there is evidence to show that early Christian commentators interpreted the culpability of this act to lie with Adam,[343] Eve soon became the central figure in this primeval act of disobedience:

> I permit no woman to teach or to have authority over a man; she is to keep silent. For Adam was formed first, then Eve; and Adam was not deceived, but the woman was deceived and became a transgressor. Yet she will be saved through child-bearing, provided they continue in faith and love and holiness, with modesty.
>
> (1 Tim. 2.12–15)

Christian theology invested Eve with a unique position, not only regarding the Fall, but also in the theology of redemption. She became the representative and type of all women, so that even the Blessed Virgin Mary was interpreted as the New Eve as Christ was the New Adam. The figure of Eve lies at the heart of Christianity's understanding and estimation of women. In contemporary Christian theological debate she deserves the closest attention of anyone who wishes either to revise that estimation of women or to uphold it.

It is possible to characterize three types of argument in Christian theology regarding Eve. These, although distinctive, are interrelated and to some extent interdependent through the biblical proof-texts

they share and the conclusions they reach.[344] The first argument
supports the notion that in gender terms a hierarchy exists in which
women are the second sex. It is founded on the order of creation
described in Gen. 2 where the text can suggest that Eve is created
after Adam and for Adam's needs: 'Then the Lord God said, "It is
not good that man should be alone; I will make him a helper fit for
him"' (Gen. 2.18). In Christian theology this verse became the
proof-text for maintaining a sexual hierarchy in the Christian family
and in ecclesiastical office. The Genesis account of the order of
creation was used in our earliest accounts of Christianity, the Pauline
epistles, to define the position of women. Two of these texts, 1 Cor.
11.7ff. and 1 Tim. 2.13, most clearly bring to mind the Genesis text.
In 1 Corinthians 11 Paul attempts to persuade the women in the
congregation not to reveal their hair while leading prayers or
prophesying,[345] 'For a man ought not to cover his head, since he is
the image and glory of God; but woman is the glory of man. (For
man was not made from woman, but woman from man. Neither was
man created for woman, but woman for man.)' (1 Cor. 11.7–9). This
passage relates to a particular problem regarding a particular Christian community at a particular time in history, but since it is part of
the Christian canon of scripture it has been recognized by churches
as normative throughout the centuries. One conclusion deduced
from this passage, that women did not bear the image of God in an
identical way or proportion to that of men, was, perhaps, the most
influential in Christianity's deliberate determining of the male gender
as normative. John Chrysostom, writing in the fourth century, for
example, interprets this passage to imply that women lost their divine
image as a result of the 'Fall'. He notes that the Greek word *exousia*,
usually translated 'veil' in 1 Cor. 11.10, actually means 'authority'
which is something that women lack since God made them sub-
servient to men as punishment for Eve's disobedience:

> For the 'image' is not meant in regard to essence, but in regard
> to authority, as we shall make clear by bringing forth argu-
> ments in an orderly manner. To grasp the point that the form
> of man is not that of God, listen to what Paul says: 'For the
> man ought not to be veiled, for he is the image and glory of
> God. But woman is the glory of man. Therefore she ought to
> have a veil (Greek: "authority") on her head'. Indeed if Paul
> here says this was the 'image', making clear the unchangeable-
> ness of the form that is patterned on God, then man is called

the 'image of God' because God has stamped him in this way. Not so, according to our opponents, who argue that not only the man must have the 'image', but the woman as well. Our answer is that the man and the woman do have one form, one distinctive character, one likeness. Then why is the man said to be in the 'image of God' and the woman not? Because what Paul says about the 'image' does not pertain to form. The 'image' has rather to do with authority, and this only the man has; the woman has it no longer. For he is subjected to no one, while she is subjected to him; as God said, 'Your inclination shall be for your husband and he shall rule over you' (Gen. 3.16). Therefore the man is in the 'image of God' since he had no one above him, just as God has no superior but rules over everything. The woman, however, is 'the glory of man', since she is subjected to him.[346]

This type of argument ensures that sexual hierarchy becomes an essential part of Christian theology. Not only is Eve the second sex because she was created after Adam, but through her disobedience she is distinct from men in that she no longer shares God's image.

The other Pauline passage, 1 Timothy 2, makes the same two points about women by declaring first that 'Adam was formed first, then Eve', and then reinforcing the concept of the 'second sex' by mentioning her disobedience. By setting out these arguments in a passage which is about ecclesiastical organization, the idea of women assuming any significant role within the power hierarchy is not viable.

New Testament scholars are divided on the question of the Pauline authorship of 1 Timothy.[347] Fiorenza seeks to understand them as late first-century attempts by Christian communities to conform to the norms of their Greco-Roman context, and notes the influence of Aristotle's ideas, of sexual hierarchy and domestic and political hierarchy.[348] One of the most important features of her work is the insistence that such texts must be read 'against the grain': such strongly worded admonitions are themselves evidence that there were situations where women were teaching men and asserting authority outside their proper domestic sphere.

When these admonitions were taken alongside the sexual hierarchy reflected in the New Testament's household codes (e.g. 'Wives, be subject to your husbands, as to the Lord' Eph. 5.22),[349] the Church Fathers had firm scriptural foundations for developing a Christian attitude to womankind that was in sympathy with tendencies in Greco-Roman culture to preserve and disseminate Aristotelian values. Augustine, for example, puzzles over the very creation of woman: what was the point of God creating such a creature? Does the description of woman as man's 'helper' (Gen. 2.18) imply that she would help the man with manual labour?[350] In fact he dismisses this since, before the Fall, such hard labour did not exist, and, furthermore, if God had wanted a manual labourer, then another man would have been more suitable. He continues:

> One can also posit that the reason for her creation as a helper had to do with the companionship she could provide for the man, if perhaps he got bored with his solitude. Yet for company and conversation, how much more agreeable it is for two male friends to dwell together than for a man and woman![351]

His eventual answer to the problem of why women were created at all is based on his view of the order of creation in which women are by nature subordinate to men:

> If it is necessary for one of two people living together to rule and the other to obey so that an opposition of wills does not disturb their peaceful cohabitation, then nothing is missing from the order we see in Genesis directed to this restraint, for one person was created before, the other afterwards, and most significantly, the latter was created from the former, the woman from the man. And nobody wants to suggest, does he, that God, if he so willed, could only make a woman from a man's side, yet that he couldn't create a man as well? I cannot think of any reason for woman's being made as man's helper, if we dismiss the reason of procreation.

Procreation, then, for Augustine, was the only valid reason behind God's decision to create woman, and the ultimate peak in this process comes when a unique woman, without tarnish of sin, brings forth the Christ child into the world.

This concept of a 'natural order' among the sexes reflects basic Aristotelian concepts:

> There are by nature various classes of rulers and ruled. For the free rules the slave, the male the female, the man the child in a different way. And all possess the various parts of the soul but possess them in different ways; for the slave has not got the

deliberative part at all, and the female has it but without full authority, while the child has it but in an undeveloped form.

(*Politics* I.1260a)[352]

John Chrysostom applies this natural order of the sexes some centuries later:

> Our life is customarily organized into two spheres: public affairs and private matters, both of which are determined by God. To woman is assigned the presidency of the household; to man, all the business of state, the marketplace, the administration of justice, government, the military, and all other such enterprises. . . . Indeed, this is a work of God's love and wisdom, that he who is skilled at the greater things is downright inept and useless in the performance of the less important ones, so that the woman's service is necessary. For if the man were adapted to undertake both sorts of activities, the female sex could easily be despised. Conversely, if the more important, more beneficial concerns were turned over to the woman, she would go quite mad.[353]

The combination of the Aristotelian notion of the natural order of things with the Genesis account of the creation of male and female furnished Christianity with the theoretical underpinning of its practice of sexual hierarchy.

The second type of argument characteristic of Christian theology about Eve concerns her particular responsibility for introducing sin into the world. This belief that the 'Fall' of the human race came about through Eve's act of eating the fruit of the tree in the 'midst of the Garden' (Gen. 3.6) can be found in Christian writing from as early as the New Testament period.[354] The first evidence we find of Eve being deemed uniquely culpable is in Paul's letter to the Corinthians: 'But I am afraid that as the serpent deceived Eve by his cunning, your thoughts will be led astray from a sincere and pure devotion to Christ' (2 Cor. 11.3). This observation of Eve's vulnerability later becomes a pronouncement of her guilt: 'Adam was not deceived, but the woman was deceived and became a transgressor' (1 Tim. 2.14). The argument for female subordination based on the order of creation is now overtaken by the belief that woman is the originator of sin. This one passage from a short epistle became the foundation text in Christian theology about women and their role and status in the church. In it the figure of Eve is of central importance: she is the first sinner and she is also the embodiment of all womankind. It would seem that her sin was so great that she and the rest of womankind even fall outside the redemptive power of Christ. Salvation for them comes through child-bearing and modest dress and behaviour rather than through the Christian soteriological scheme of the death and resurrection of the Son of God. The theology of this verse was certainly one factor in Augustine's belief, quoted above, that the only reason for woman's existence was procreation.

We find the same attitude regarding the necessity for modesty amongst Eve and her daughters expressed by the late second-century Christian writer Tertullian. He begins his discourse *On the Dress of Women* as follows:

> If such strong faith remained on earth, as strong as the reward of faith is expected in heaven, not one of you, dearest sisters, from the time she acknowledged the living God and learned about herself, that is, about the condition of women, would have desired a more charming dress, not to speak of a more exquisite one. She would rather go about in cheap clothes and strive for an appearance characterised by neglect. She would carry herself around like Eve, mourning and penitent, that she might more fully expiate by each garment of penitence that which she acquired from Eve – I mean the degradation of the first sin and the hatefulness of human perdition. 'In pains and anxieties you bring forth children, woman, and your inclination is for your husband, and he rules over you' (Gen. 3.16) – and you know not that you also are an Eve?
>
> (I,1,1)

As in the case of the passage from 1 Timothy, Tertullian steeps his arguments in material from Genesis 3; and, again like the writer of 1 Timothy, sees Eve as 'everywoman':

> God's judgment on this sex lives on in our age; the guilt necessarily lives on as well. You are the Devil's gateway; you are the unsealer of that tree; you are the first foresaker of the divine law; you are the one who persuaded him whom the Devil was not brave enough to approach; you so lightly crushed the image of God, the man Adam; because of your punishment, that is death, even the Son of God had to die. And you think to adorn yourself beyond your 'tunics of skins' (Gen. 3.21)?
>
> (I,1,2)

154

Here the female gender has a particular responsibility not only for the first sin, but also for the death of Christ. The more one particular interpretation of Genesis 3 became embedded in Christian theology, the more marginalized from the heart of that religion women became. They came to be identified with the 'other', in opposition to the normative male gender which had now been perfected in the incarnation of the divine into human male form.[355]

In the century following Tertullian, both Ambrose and Augustine echo and reinforce the theological basis of sexual hierarchy through the belief in Eve's primary responsibility for the Fall, constantly referring back to the words of 1 Timothy. First Ambrose: 'The woman, therefore, is the originator of the man's wrongdoing, not the man's of the woman's. Hence Paul says, "Adam was not deceived, but the woman was deceived and committed sin" (1 Tim. 2.14).'[356] And then Augustine:

> The apostle Paul's words were not meaningless when he said, 'For Adam was formed first, then Eve. And Adam was not led astray, but the woman was, and was made guilty of transgression' (1 Tim. 2.13–14), i.e., that through her the man became guilty of transgression. For the apostle calls him a transgressor as well when he says, 'In the likeness of the transgression of Adam, who is a figure of him who is to come' (Rom. 5.14), but he does not say that Adam was 'led astray'. For even when asked, Adam does not reply, 'The woman whom you gave me led me astray and I ate,' but rather he says, 'She gave me from the tree and I ate.' She, to be sure, did speak the words, 'The serpent led me astray'.
>
> (Gen. 3.13)[357]

In this comment, comparing Adam with Eve, we see how Augustine singles the woman out as having particular responsibility for the Fall. Although Adam is not without sin, he was not 'led astray'.

A third line of argument addressed by early Christianity to the figure of Eve concerned her typological link with Mary, the mother of Jesus. This link can be traced to as early as the middle of the second century in the work of Justin Martyr. Towards the end of that century Irenaeus, Bishop of Lyons, discussed the similarities and contrasts between these two women. Having noted first how Eve shares the same status as Mary in having a husband and yet remaining a virgin, he continues:

Eve, having become disobedient, was made the cause of death both for herself and for all the human race. Thus also Mary had a husband selected for her and nonetheless was a virgin, yet by her obedience she was made the cause of salvation both for herself and for all the human race. For this reason the law calls a woman engaged to a man his wife, while conceding that she is still a virgin. This indicates a link that goes from Mary back to Eve.

. . . Moreover, the knot of Eve's disobedience was loosened through the obedience of Mary. For what the virgin Eve bound through unbelief, this the Virgin Mary loosed through faith.[358]

Mary's faith is expressed in her affirmation of God's intention to make her, a virgin, conceive the Christ child: 'Behold, I am the handmaid of the Lord; let it be to me according to your word' (Lk. 1.38).

Although evidence identifying Mary as the New Eve is not explicit in the New Testament, the Church Fathers found texts to support their typology, for example, the contrasting imagery of the Whore of Babylon (Rev.17) and the Queen of Heaven (Rev.12) in the *Book of Revelation*.

In considering the negative interpretations of Eve that lie at the heart of Christianity, we must note that there is also a certain ambivalence concerning her sin. Although, in Christian terms, it led to the 'Fall', and is the greatest sin ever committed, without it there would have been no act of redemption. Eve and Mary are both central characters in ensuring the inevitability of Christ's redemptive work, and Christianity recognizes a bond between these two women in their cooperation in bringing about the birth of Christ. Eve is then the type of the one that is to come: Mary. This is evident in Jerome's Vulgate version of Gen. 3.15b where God castigates the serpent. The Hebrew is rendered in English as follows: 'he [Hebrew *hu*] shall bruise your head, and you shall bruise his heel.' But Jerome has the feminine: 'She it is who shall bruise your head' (*ipsa conteret caput tuum*). In the repercussions of Eve's act of disobedience is found the promise of redemption through the act of another woman.[359]

Christianity produced two types to represent all of womankind: Eve and Mary. In reality Mary was the one and only example of her type, and all women were daughters of Eve. As Augustine defined his concept of Original Sin, identifying concupiscence as the primary cause and Eve as its source and instigator, so Mary became more and more elevated in her unique status. As the drastic consequences of Eve's sinful disobedience became apparent, her sinful nature was laid bare to stand in stark contrast to the perfect, untainted nature of Mary.

With the concept of congenital sin came speculation on the possible sinlessness of Christ, and by degree, the sinlessness of his mother. If Christ was to be without taint of congenital sin then his mother had to be without sin. The moment that sin is passed on from one generation to another, according to Augustine, is the moment during the act of sex when conception takes place. It can be recognized by the lust that accompanies all such acts. It is woman who awakens this lust in man, just as Eve had sparked off Adam's lust for the fruit of the tree in the midst of the Garden. Christ's conception bypassed this process and was therefore devoid of concupiscence. Mary's own immaculate conception meant that she also bypassed the inheritance of sin and therefore could not pass any stain on to the son in her womb.

To conclude, within Christian theology as expressed in its first centuries, two theories of gender are apparent. The first, noted in the charismatic organization of the Jesus movement and the first urban communities, manifests Plato's vision of the *grove of academe*, where equality of opportunity allows for the development and inclusion of both genders.[360] The second, resting on the Aristotelian notion of natural order, not only makes sexual hierarchy visible both in the domestic and public spheres, but also adds theological underpinning through reflection on the implications of Eve's sin in order to ensure a uniformity of belief and practice in the universal church. We noted at the beginning of this section on Christianity that this tradition was distinctive in comparison to Greco-Roman cults and Judaism in its explicit articulation of the nature and roles of male and female. In this context it is more useful to set Christianity beside classical Aristotelian and Platonic philosophy which did concern itself with the meaning of matter formed as male and female.[361] Such a study falls outside the limits of this project, allowing us only to note that from its earliest days Christianity identified itself as a religion that presumed to regulate for every aspect of life and thought for the individual, the community and, eventually, the Empire.

EPILOGUE

This study has brought together an array of divergent images of women and their experiences in the context of ancient religion. It has shown how such images defy categorization or generalization, and how any boundaries that did exist were challenged by contrary practice or belief. We described this period of the late Republic and early Empire as one of 'pre-traditionalization' in an attempt both to express the nature of its plurality, and to construct a bridge between that ancient context and our own, which may in turn be described in terms of 'post-traditionalization'. Between the two lies Christianity, the tradition that has dominated western civilization, and its colonial outposts, for nearly two millennia.

The lasting impression of any study that has examined women and how they have been perceived in the religious contexts of the ancient world is one of diversity: diversity of religious systems, and diversity within those systems. A similar diversity is being encountered in the west today where traditional religion and values have been usurped from their metaphysical plane of truth by the challenges posed by post-modernity. The phenomenon of new age religion, characterized by numerous new religious movements, tempts us to make comparisons with the pre-traditionalized former age before the intervention of the monolithic influence of Christianity. The new age religions that attempt to rediscover past traditions, for example the New Pagans, the Wicca movement, goddess spirituality, perhaps correspond to the enthusiasm found in Rome in pre-Christian times for ancient oriental myths and cults. In the context of new age religion women are shaping religion for themselves. Their symbols reflect what is distinctive to their varied experience of what constitutes being female on the fluid spectrum of gender. Today in the context of goddess spirituality we can encounter Demeter and Persephone

158

anew; Lilith, too, can roam free once more; and Eve, rediscovered and washed clean of the world's sinful conscience, can be seen as a means of enlightenment.[362]

NOTES

1 Description of Zenobia, Queen of Palmyra composed in the late third century CE, from *Scriptores Historiae Augustae: Thirty Pretenders*, 30.13–18; translation, D. Magie, Loeb Classical Library, Cambridge, Mass., Harvard University Press, 1967–1968.

2 John Chrysostom, *The Kind of Women Who Ought to be Taken as Wives* 4; translation, E.A. Clark, *Women in the Early Church*, Lewiston, NY, Edwin Mellen, 1984, pp.36–37.

3 See below, pp.7–8.

4 From Mary Beard's review of R. Kraemer, *Her Share of the Blessings: Women's Religions Among Pagans, Jews, and Christians in the Greco-Roman World*, Oxford, Oxford University Press, 1992, in *London Review of Books*, 13 May 1993.

5 The following studies are interdisciplinary, as well as Simone de Beauvoir's classic analysis, *The Second Sex*, London, Picador, 1949/1988: D.L. Rhode (ed.), *Theoretical Perspectives on Sexual Difference*, New Haven, Yale University Press, 1990; J.A. Doyle and M.A. Paludi, *Sex and Gender: The Human Experience*, 2nd ed., Dubuque, Iowa, William C. Brown Publishers, 1991.

6 See below, pp.110–112.

7 Critiques of endemic dualism have always characterized feminism; today they proliferate in the context of eco-feminism. See, e.g., R.R. Ruether, *Gaia and God: An Ecofeminist Theology of Earth Healing*, London, SCM Press, 1992. Conversely, for a collection of positive feminist notions of difference see N. Schoer and E. Weed (eds), *The Essential Difference*, Bloomington and Indianapolis, Indiana University Press, 1994.

8 For a systematic appraisal of Plato's views on women's nature and status see T.J.Saunders, 'Plato on Women in the Laws', in A.Powell (ed.), *The Greek World*, 2nd ed., London, Routledge, 1995, pp.591–609.

9 Saunders,'Plato on Women', pp.602–603.

10 *Laws*, 694de; 731d; 790ab; 817c; 909e; also *Timaeus*, 42a–d; 90e–91d. Discussed in Saunders, 'Plato on Women', p.592.

11 See above, p.3.

12 For an account of the recent adoption of notions of 'difference' in positive terms in feminist theory see E. Graham, *Making the Difference: Gender, Personhood and Theology*, London, Mowbray, 1995, pp.169–191.

13 This point provides a focus for debate among feminists, between those who argue for an essential 'woman's' experience (M. Daly, *Beyond God the Father: Toward a Philosophy of Women's Liberation*, Boston, Beacon Press, 1973); and those who argue for diversity stemming from race, context and class (Audre Lorde, 'The Master's Tools Will Never Dismantle the Master's House', in C. Moraga and G. Anzaldua (eds), *This Bridge Called My Back: Writings by Radical Women of Color*, Watertown, MA, Persephone Press, 1981, pp.95–105).

14 See above, p.4.

15 See Tacitus, *Annals*, 15.44.

16 Definitions given in C.T. Lewis and C. Short, *A Latin Dictionary*, Oxford, Oxford University Press, 1879.

17 Note *Sirach*, probably written in Greek and then translated into Hebrew.

18 *On the Generation of Animals*, 4.6; see the discussion of Aristotle in M.R. Lefkowitz and M.B. Fant, *Women's Lives in Greece and Rome: A Source Book in Translation*, Baltimore, Johns Hopkins University Press, 1982.

19 For an extended account of issues relating to women, family and sexuality in the age of Augustus and the Julio-Claudians see E. Fantham *et al.* (eds), *Women in the Classical World*, Oxford, Oxford University Press, 1994, pp.294–327.

20 See J.P.V.D. Balsdon, *Roman Women: Their History and Habits*, London, The Bodley Head, 1962, p.75.

21 As described in para. 9 of Livy's *History*, written *circa* 28 BCE: 'For we have now reached a point where our degeneracy is intolerable – and so are the measures by which alone it can be reformed.'

22 A more realistic assessment of this legislation can be found in Beryl Rawson's 'The Roman Family', in *The Family in Ancient Rome: New Perspectives*, London, Routledge, 1992, pp.1–57.

23 For a full description of these ancient forms of marriage, see Balsdon, *Roman Women*, pp.179–180. One of these ancient forms, *confarreatio*, had a highly religious nature and was characterized by being indissoluble.

24 F. Schulz, *Classical Roman Law*, Oxford, Oxford University Press, 1951, part 2, p.103, sect.180.

25 Livy, *Periochae* 59; Suetonius, *Divus Augustus* 89.

26 A clear account of the legal status of women during this period and beyond can be found in John K. Evans, *War, Women and Children in Ancient Rome*, London, Routledge, 1991, pp.7–49.

27 Evans, *War, Women and Children*, p.9; see also pp.21–22 which raise the possibility that this attitude was, in fact, imported into Roman law from Hellenistic thought, particularly that of Aristotle.

28 See above, p.19.

29 Recorded by Gaius, *Institutiones*, 1,108 sq.

30 Discussed by Evans, *War, Women and Children*, pp.11–13.

31 Evans, *War, Women and Children*, p.13.

32 See below, pp.68–70 and pp. 126–129.

33 See above, p.19.

34 See above, p.18.

35 For details of further legislation see Evans, *War, Women and Children*, pp.13–17.
36 Mentioned in Balsdon, *Roman Women*, p.276.
37 See above, p.18.
38 See, respectively, Tacitus, *Agricola* 4; Plutarch, *Tiberius Gracchus* 1 and below p. 25; Tacitus, *Dialogus* 28.
39 *The Roman Mother*, London, Routledge, 1990, p.143.
40 Beryl Rawson (ed.), *The Family in Ancient Rome*, p.40.
41 Livy, 34.2ff.
42 Livy, 34.2–4.
43 For a summary of the argument about its authenticity see Balsdon, *Roman Women*, p.293, n.35.
44 Translation from Balsdon, *Roman Women*, p.34.
45 Translation from Balsdon, *Roman Women*, p.35.
46 Appian, *Bella Civilia*, 4.32–34; discussed in J.P. Hallet, *Fathers and Daughters in Roman Society*, Princeton, Princeton University Press, 1984, pp.58–59.
47 This theory is discussed by Evans, *War, Women and Children*, pp.20–22.
48 Recorded in Livy 34.3.9.
49 See below, pp.55–56.
50 From Polybius, 31.26.3–5; quoted in Evans, *War, Women and Children*, p.36.
51 Balsdon's translation, *Roman Women*, p.48 (*Coniuratio Catilinae* 24.3–25).
52 Evans, *War, Women and Children*, p.84.
53 *ibid.*; quoting from Valerius Maximus 4.4.
54 See, for example, Evans' account of legislation limiting the number of guests and the amount of food and wine allowed at banquets, *War, Women and Children*, pp.67–68. Evans notes that the frequency of amendments to this legislation reflects the problems encountered in enforcing it.
55 *Goddesses, Whores, Wives and Slaves: Women in Classical Antiquity*, New York, Shocken Books, 1975, pp.181ff.
56 *Aulularia*, 167–169; quoted in Evans, *War, Women and Children*, pp.64–65.
57 An account of him can be found in Suetonius, *De Grammaticis* 23.
58 Evans, *War, Women and Children*, pp.101–117, discusses the rural situation for lower class women in some detail and with useful illustrations.
59 *Bellum Iugurthinum*, 41.7–8; translation, Evans, *War, Women and Children*, p.107.
60 *De Re Rustica*, 12.4–5; translation, Evans, *War, Women and Children*, p.115.
61 See, e.g., *De Re Rustica*, 12.3.8; also, writing two centuries earlier, Cato, *De Agricultura*, 143.2; Plautus, *Mercator*, 397.
62 See N.Kampen, *Image and Status: Roman Working Women in Ostia*, Berlin, Mann, 1981, for a full discussion of the types of employment open to women.
63 See *ibid.*, pp.126–127.

64 Evans, *War, Women and Children*, pp.130–142, lists numerous pieces of evidence from texts and inscriptions of the late Republic and early Empire of women being employed in entertainment.
65 See Horace, *Satirae*, 1.2.57–59.
66 See inscriptions *CIL* (*Corpus Inscriptionum Latinarum*), IV.1507, 1510; 8185.
67 Evidenced in Horace, *Epistulae*, 1.15.21; Dio Chrysostomus, *Orationes*, 5.25.
68 In one temple alone, that of Aphrodite, there were reputed to be a thousand prostitutes, see Strabo 8.6.20; and Aulus Gellius, *Noctes Atticae*, 1.8. Mid-first-century CE Christian sources also record the lively trade of prostitution in Corinth, see 1 Cor. 6.
69 See, e.g., Horace, *Satirae*, 1.2.3; Petronius, *Satyricon*, 7; Plautus, *Poenulus*, 265–270. For a list of relevant graffiti from Pompeii, see Evans, *War, Women and Children*, p.162, n.137.
70 For an attempt to contextualize Judaism at this time, see above, pp.14–15.
71 At the beginning of the first century BCE the notion of scripture in Judaism included the Torah and Prophets; this can be evidenced from the New Testament, as well as Jewish texts. The Mishnah, the first codification of Jewish practice and belief, was complete by 200 CE. The most influential texts for Judaism, the Talmudim, were finally edited in the fifth century CE. These dates are irrelevant in the sense that certain material within the Mishnah and Talmudim dates from before the first century CE. For a contemporary view of Jewish texts see J. Neusner, *Introduction to Rabbinic Literature*, New York, Doubleday, 1994; on dating Jewish texts and the problems associated with it see pp.651–668.
72 For a full and convincing picture of Judaism in this period see E. Schürer, *The History of the Jewish People in the Age of Jesus Christ*, 4 vols, revised and edited by G. Vermes *et al.*, Edinburgh, T & T Clark, 1973–1986.
73 The Mishnah forms the nucleus of the Oral Torah, and its interpretation is the material contained in the Bavli and Palestinian Talmudim, as well as the Tosephta, and the many other collections of midrash, that is, Jewish exegesis, e.g. Midrash Rabbah. For a full account of the types and content of ancient Jewish texts, see H.L. Strack, *Introduction to the Talmud and Midrash*, New York, Atheneum, 1969, and J. Neusner, *Introduction to Rabbinic Literature*.
74 For a full historical account of Roman/Jewish political relations see revised Schürer, *History of the Jewish People*, Vol.1, pp.243–557.
75 See, e.g., Josephus, *Ant.* xiv 16.4; *War* v 13.6; Philo, *Legat.* 37.
76 Vol.II (1979), p.313.
77 See above, p.15.
78 Recorded by Josephus, *Ant.*, xiv 10 (185–267); xvi 6 (160–179); Philo also attests to this situation in the time of Augustus, *Legat.* 23 (156–157).
79 In *pro Flacco* 28/67.
80 *Symposium* iv 5.
81 *Sat.* vi 160.
82 Fergus Millar in revised Schürer, *History of the Jewish People*, Vol.IIIi, p.153.
83 E.P. Sanders, *Judaism: Practice and Belief 63* BCE-66 CE, London, SCM

Press, 1992, provides a convincing study of Judaism in Palestine from the conquest of Pompey to the beginning of the Jewish revolt.

84 Gen. 17.10–14 and Lev. 12.3.

85 See Leonie Archer, *Her Price Beyond Rubies*, Sheffield, Sheffield Academic Press, 1990, pp.110–122.

86 *Spec.Leg.* 3.169.

87 See below, pp.81–82.

88 For contemporary discussions of the menstrual taboo in Israelite and Jewish society see J. Neusner, *The Idea of Purity in Ancient Judaism, with critique and commentary by M. Douglas*, Leiden, Brill, 1973; L.J. Archer, 'Bound by Blood: Circumcision and Menstrual Taboo in Post Exilic Judaism', in J. Martin-Soskice (ed.), *After Eve: Women, Theology and Judaeo-Christian Tradition*, London, Marshall Pickering, 1989; B.Greenburg, 'Female Sexuality and Bodily Functions in the Jewish Tradition', in J. Becher (ed.), *Women, Religion and Sexuality*, Geneva, WCC Publications, 1990, pp.1–44; P.N. Levinson, 'Women and Sexuality: Traditions and Progress', in *ibid.*, pp.45–63.

89 See above, pp.15–17 and p.89.

90 In a forthcoming article, 'A Note on Leviticus 12.5', Jonathan Magonet argues that the disparity between the period of uncleanness after a male and female child can be explained more convincingly through the medical evidence of menstruating female babies than the values of patriarchy. He argues that the common occurrence of female babies having 'mini' periods at birth prompted the rabbis to regard them as menstruants and therefore allowed for two periods of menstrual impurity, one for the mother and one for the daughter.

91 Deut. 22.28–29.

92 Deut. 22.26.

93 Deut. 22.20–21.

94 Deut. 22.15–17.

95 Deut. 22.19.

96 Deut. 22.19.

97 See below, pp.132–134, and pp.136–137.

98 For a fuller discussion of this text in the context of the status of women see D.F. Sawyer, 'Resurrecting Eve', in P. Morris and D.F. Sawyer (eds), *A Walk in the Garden*, Sheffield, Sheffield Academic Press, 1992, pp.273–289, also below, pp. 55–56.

99 The situation of women in Greco-Roman Palestine is studied in detail by Archer, *Her Price Beyond Rubies*.

100 See below, pp.79–81.

101 See below, pp.117–157.

102 For an analysis of early Christianity being defined as a new religious movement, see J.T. Sanders, *Schismatics, Sectarians, Dissidents, Deviants: The First One Hundred Years of Jewish–Christian Relations*, London, SCM Press, 1993, pp.242–257.

103 For well-documented accounts of earliest Christianity see C.C. Rowland, *Christian Origins*, London, SPCK, 1985; N.T. Wright, *The New Testament and the People of God*, Vol.1, London, SPCK, 1993.

104 See the comment made by the Roman historian Suetonius, mentioned below, p.174, note 34.
105 For a discussion of these charismatic gifts, see below, p.92–93.
106 See below, pp.75–76.
107 Fergus Millar, in revised Schürer, *History of the Jewish People*, Vol.IIIi, pp.160–161; for a detailed account of the evidence supporting this comment see pp.159–176.
108 For a recent and accessible account of the dating of New Testament texts see the chart in R.E. Brown *et al.*, *The New Jerome Biblical Commentary*, London, Geoffrey Chapman, 1991, p.1045.
109 See above, pp.74–80.
110 *Theology and Feminism*, Oxford, Blackwell, 1990.
111 The work we will be drawing on most frequently in these sections is her book, *In Memory of Her: A Feminist Theological Reconstruction of Christian Origins*, London, SCM Press, 1983.
112 K. Dowden, *Religion and the Romans*, London, Bristol Classical Press, 1992, p.8.
113 In M. Beard and J. North (eds), *Pagan Priests: Religion and Power in the Ancient World*, London, Duckworth, 1990, p.250.
114 See below, pp.66–68.
115 See, e.g. Fiorenza, *In Memory of Her*, pp.245–342, which includes discussion of Aristotle in relation to the developing structures and ideas relating to women in some Christian communities in the last third of the first century CE.
116 A recent thorough-going study of the function and status of pagan priests from the time of the Republic to the Empire has been produced by Beard and North (eds), *Pagan Priests*. This situation is challenged by the practices of the Magna Mater cult, see below, pp.122–126.
117 Richard Gordon in Beard and North (eds), *Pagan Priests*, p.231.
118 Dowden, *Religion and the Romans*, discusses this procedure, pp.32–33.
119 Translation, *ibid.*
120 See above, pp.15–17.
121 For a recent account of the Amazons see Fantham *et al.*, *Women in the Classical World*, pp.128–135.
122 *ibid.*, p.131.
123 Here this concept of the Amazons was explicitly challenging the demarcation of gender roles in the classical world; for further illustrations of this see below, pp.119–129.
124 The persistence of the Amazon women in classical records, some purporting to be historical, might set them more accurately in the category of legend rather than myth.
125 For a recent excursus on Spartan women see Fantham *et al.*, *Women in the Classical World*, pp.56–67.
126 See below, pp.110–113.
127 See, e.g., Fantham *et al.*, *Women in the Classical World*, p.63.
128 Translation, E.C. Marchant and G.W. Bowersock, *Xenophon VII. Scripta Minora*, Loeb Classical Library, Cambridge, Mass., Harvard University Press, 1968.

NOTES

129 See R. Talbert, *Plutarch on Sparta*, Penguin, London, 1988.

130 Translation of Aristotle's *Politics*: H. Rackham, Loeb Classical Library, Cambridge, Mass., Harvard University Press, 1926.

131 Fantham *et al.*, *Women in the Classical World*, pp.12–17.

132 Translation, Jane Snyder, *The Woman and the Lyre: Women Writers in Classical Greece and Rome*, Carbondale, Southern Illinois University Press, 1989.

133 Translation, Snyder, *The Woman and the Lyre*.

134 Kraemer, *Her Share*, p. 25; Marilyn B. Arthur, 'Politics and Pomegranates: An Interpretation of the Homeric Hymn to Demeter', *Arethusa*, 10 (1977), 7–47.

135 Bruce Lincoln, *Emerging from the Chrysalis: Studies in Rituals of Women's Initiation*, Cambridge, Mass., Harvard University Press, 1981, pp.71–90.

136 Kraemer, *Her Share*, p.25.

137 Kraemer, *Her Share*, pp.22–29.

138 For a full description of the lives of women in classical Athens, which illustrates these points, see Fantham *et al.*, *Women in the Classical World*, pp.68–127.

139 Frag. 524N [583R]; this translation, Helene P. Foley in Fantham *et al.*, *Women in the Classical World*, p.70.

140 A similar role could be argued for Aristotle's ideas which were popular in the same context. See above, p.55.

141 Kraemer, *Her Share*, p.29.

142 *ibid.*, p.30.

143 Translation, Helen P. Foley, in Fantham *et al.*, *Women in the Classical World*, pp.90–91.

144 Three examples are: Apollodorus, *Library*, 3.4.2–3; Diodorus, 3.62–74; and Philostratus, *Apollonios*, 2.9.

145 *Women in the Classical World* contains a particularly useful collection of photographs of these.

146 See Susan Cole Guettel, 'New Evidence for the Mysteries of Dionysus', *GRBS*, 21 (1980) 3, 223–238.

147 Kraemer, *Her Share*, p.39.

148 *On the First Cold*, 18, and *Bravery of Women*, 13. Also, Pausanius, *Description*, 10.4.3, describing his travels in Greece during the second century BCE, mentions women called Thyiades who, with women from Delphi, celebrated rites to Dionysus on Mount Parnassus.

149 *Annals*, 39.8–19.

150 See pp. 22–24, above where Cato's contribution to the Oppian Law debate is discussed.

151 See above, p.14.

152 Balsdon, *Roman Women*, pp.32–33.

153 This sketch of the story is based on *Livy*, 39.9.2–14.3.

154 See the controversy over the style of women's hair among the Christians in Corinth in the mid-first century CE, below, pp.103–105, and the wild hair of the *galli* priests, below, pp.122–124.

155 See the discussion in Kraemer, *Her Share*, pp.43–44.

166

156 See below, pp.119–126.
157 Plutarch, *On Isis and Osiris*, was familiar with the cult through his acquaintance, Clea, a priestess of Isis.
158 Fantham *et al.*, *Women in the Classical World*, p.154.
159 *Metamorphosis*, 11.8–17; translation, R.Graves, *The Transformations of Lucius otherwise known as the Golden Ass, by Apuleius*, New York, Farrer Straus, 1951.
160 Discussed in Fantham *et al.*, *Women in the Classical World*, pp.342–343.
161 Sharon Kelly Heyob, *The Cult of Isis among Women in the Greco-Roman World*, Leiden, Brill, 1975.
162 Balsdon, *Roman Women*, p.235.
163 'The Sexual Status of Vestal Virgins', *Journal of Roman Studies*, 70 (1980), 12–27.
164 This and the following extracts are taken from Plutarch, *Numa* 10. Translation, R. Warner, in E. Fuller (ed.), *Plutarch: Lives of the Noble Romans*, London, Penguin, 1959, pp.49–50.
165 Fantham *et al.*, *Women in the Classical World*, p.235.
166 See Balsdon, *Roman Women*, pp.235–243, for a lively and full account of the lifestyle of the Vestal Virgins. The interpretation given with the description needs to be read with other material, particularly Beard, 'The Sexual Status of Vestal Virgins'. See also below, pp.127–129.
167 This comment appears in Mary Beard's review of Kraemer, *Her Share*, in *London Review of Books*, 13 May 1993. See also Beard, 'Vestal Virgins'; for more detailed discussion of the Magna Mater cult, see below, pp.119–126.
168 For a well-documented account of the Roman *matronae* see Kraemer, *Her Share*, pp.50–70.
169 This group had been particularly instrumental in the repeal of the Oppian Law; see above, pp.22–26.
170 For a full study of this issue see H.H.J. Brouwer, *Bona Dea: The Sources and a Description of the Cult*, EPRO 110, Leiden, Brill, 1989.
171 *Satire*, 6.
172 See, e.g., Lev.21–22; and above, pp.36–38.
173 Josephus, writing in the first century CE, gives a full description of the temple precincts, *Jewish War*, 5; cf. Mishnah Middoth.
174 Translation, Peretz Segal, 'The Penalty of the Warning Inscription from the Temple of Jerusalem', *IEJ* (*Israel Exploration Journal*, Jerusalem), 39 (1989), 79–84. This article argues that, even at the time that Jerusalem was governed by Rome directly, the priests had the authority to club such an intruder to death, cf. m.Sanh.9.6.
175 E.P. Sanders, *Judaism: Practice and Belief 63* BCE – 66 CE, London, SCM Press, 1992, p.61.
176 For an account of this and other temples at Arad, Elephantine, Araq el-Emir, and also evidence of animal sacrifice at Qumran and Sardis, see Michael Stone, *Scriptures, Sects and Visions: A Profile of Judaism from Ezra to the Jewish Revolts*, Philadelphia, Fortress, 1980. The temple at Leontopolis had been founded by Onias IV the legitimate heir to the high priesthood of Jerusalem on realizing that he would not inherit that role due to the events of the Maccabean revolt. The temple functioned

as a Jewish cultic centre from 160 BCE until 73 CE when it was closed by the Romans.

177 Brooten, *Women Leaders in the Ancient Synagogue: Inscriptional Evidence and Background Issues*, Brown Judaic Studies No.36, Atlanta, Georgia, Scholars Press, 1982, pp.73–74, and for a discussion of this inscription alongside two others that use similar language, but which could not be understood as referring to an actual cultic function for the particular woman mentioned, see pp.75–99.

178 *ibid.*, p.88.

179 *ibid.*, pp.77–95.

180 For an accessible and up-to-date bibliography on these issues see revised Schürer, *History of the Jewish People*, Vol.IIIi, pp.150–176.

181 *Hist.* v 5; translation, Millar in revised Schürer, *History of the Jewish People*, p.153.

182 See above, p.35.

183 See above, p.14.

184 Commented on by Kraemer, *Her Share*, p.71.

185 See above, pp.36–40.

186 *Hellenism – Judaism – Christianity: Essays on their Interaction*, Kampen, The Netherlands, Kok Pharos, 1994, p.80.

187 Here we would also include side rooms or curtained off sections of the main space, i.e. any section segregated from the main area of activity.

188 Brooten, *Women Leaders*, p.103; see her full critique of the available evidence for segregation of men and women in the ancient synagogues, pp.103–138; also, Sylvia Rothschild, 'Undermining the Pillars that Support the Women's Gallery', in Sybil Sheridan (ed.), *Hear Our Voice: Women Rabbis Tell their Stories*, London, SCM Press, 1994, pp.138–149.

189 See above, pp.73–74.

190 See Brooten, *Women Leaders*, pp.130–135.

191 Ex. 26ff.

192 In Philo and Josephus' descriptions of the Essenes they account for celibacy through misogyny; see, e.g., *War*, ii, 8, 12 (161).

193 *De Vita Contempl.* 32–33, and 69.

194 Brooten, *Women Leaders*, p.134.

195 See above, pp.74–75, where Brooten's work is relevant to the cultic context of Judaism.

196 Brooten, *Women Leaders*, p.1.

197 Translation from Greek, *ibid.*, p.5.

198 *ibid.*, p.10.

199 E.g., m.Yoma 7.1; m.Sota 7.7,8; Mark 5.22, 35–38; Luke 8.49.

200 Brooten, *Women Leaders*, p.31.

201 *Chattel or Person? The Status of Women in the Mishnah*, Oxford, Oxford University Press, 1988, p.155.

202 For a description of the community see, e.g., revised Schürer, *History of the Jewish People*, Vol.II, pp.575–585; for an account of their literature see the same work, Vol.IIIi, pp.380–469.

203 See this reflected in Paul's comment in 1 Cor. 1.23.

204 See, e.g., Matt.10.23; Mk 9.1; Rom. 13.11–12; 1 Cor. 15.20–28; 1 Thess. 4.15–17.
205 For a full and informed discussion of these issues see C.C. Rowland, *Christian Origins*.
206 On this contextualization of the Book of Ruth see A. LaCocque, *The Feminine Unconventional: Four Subversive Figures in Israel's Tradition*, Minneapolis, Fortress Press, 1990, pp.84–116.
207 See, e.g., P. Trible, *God and the Rhetoric of Sexuality*, Philadelphia, Fortress Press, 1979, pp.166–196; A. Brenner, *A Feminist Companion to Ruth*, Sheffield, Sheffield Academic Press, 1993.
208 See above, pp.59–61.
209 See R. Adler, 'The Virgin in the Brothel and Other Anomalies: Character and Context in the Legend of Beruria', *Tikkun*, 3.6 (1989), 28–32,102–105; also, Elizabeth Sarah, 'Beruria: A Suitable Case for Mistreatment', in S. Sheridan (ed.), *Hear Our Voice*, pp.82–98.
210 *Hear Our Voice*, pp.87–88.
211 *Women as Sources of Torah in the Rabbinic Tradition*, New York, Shocken Books, 1976, p.264.
212 See above, pp.54–55.
213 Such is the opinion of J. Wegner, 'The Image and Status of Women in Classical Rabbinic Judaism', in J. Baskin (ed.), *Jewish Women in Historical Perspective*, Detroit, Wayne State University Press, 1991, pp.63–93; see also D. Goodblatt, 'The Beruria Traditions', in W. Green (ed.), *Persons and Institutions in Early Rabbinic Judaism*, Missoula, Montana, Scholars Press, 1977, pp. 207–235.
214 See above, p.214.
215 Fiorenza, *In Memory of Her*, p.109.
216 See above, pp.42–43.
217 C.C. Rowland, *Christian Origins*, p.115.
218 See Matt. 3.13–17; Mk 1.9–11; Lk. 3.21–22; Jn 1.29–33.
219 See, e.g., Jn 16.13–14; Rom. 8.9.
220 Also, Matt. 20.26–27; Lk. 22.24–27.
221 See Fiorenza, *In Memory of Her*, pp.147–148.
222 For example Aristotle, see below, pp.111–113.
223 Fiorenza, *In Memory of Her*, p.148.
224 G.Theissen, *Sociology of Early Palestinian Christianity*, Philadelphia, Fortress, 1978.
225 See D.F. Sawyer, 'The Story of Mary: Luke's Version', in *New Blackfriars*, December 1989, pp.555–564; and R. Radford Ruether, *Sexism and God-Talk: Towards a Feminist Theology*, London, SCM Press, 1983, pp.152–158.
226 See A. Reinhartz, 'The Gospel of John', in E.S. Fiorenza (ed.), *Searching the Scriptures Volume 2: A Feminist Commentary*, London, SCM Press, 1995, pp.572–573.
227 See S.Ringe, 'A Gentile Woman's Story', in L. Russell (ed.), *Feminist Interpretation of the Bible*, Oxford, Blackwell, 1985, pp.65–72.
228 See above, pp.42–43.
229 See, e.g., Jn 11.1–53; A. Reinhartz, 'From Narrative to History: The Resurrection of Mary and Martha', in A.J. Levine (ed.), *'Women Like*

This': New Perspectives on Jewish Women in the Greco-Roman World, Atlanta, Scholars Press, 1991, pp.174–176.

230 Paul quotes from this passage in Jeremiah in Rom. 11.27 where the context is both universal and eschatological.

231 I discuss this point more fully in 'The New Adam in the Theology of St Paul', in P. Morris and D.F. Sawyer (eds), *A Walk in the Garden: Biblical, Iconographical and Literary Images of Eden*, Sheffield, Sheffield Academic Press, 1992, pp.105–116.

232 Matt. 28.1; Mk 16.1; Lk. 23.55–25.10; Jn 20.1–18.

233 See above, p.78.

234 See above, p.79 n.193.

235 L. Bennett Elder, 'Judith', in E. Schussler Fiorenza (ed.), *Searching the Scriptures Vol.2*, p.455.

236 *The Feminine Unconventional*, p.35.

237 E.g., 10.1–5.

238 *Jewish Literature Between the Bible and the Mishnah: A Historical and Literary Introduction*, Philadelphia, Fortress Press, 1981, p.108.

239 An invaluable resource for outlining the social context for the Pauline communities is Wayne Meeks, *The First Urban Christians: The Social World of the Apostle Paul*, New Haven, Yale University Press, 1983.

240 For detailed comment on the Galatians passage, its context and implications for other Pauline texts, see Fiorenza, *In Memory of Her*, pp.205–241.

241 *ibid.*, p.227.

242 Balsdon, *Roman Women*, p.256.

243 Tibullus 1.3.29–32; Fiorenza, *In Memory of Her*, p.227.

244 See the discussion of the Greco-Roman cults and myths above, pp.62–68; and below, pp.119–129.

245 This passage from 1 Cor. continues with a discussion of the creation of man and woman and will be discussed in a later chapter; see below, pp.150–151.

246 For a discussion within the contemporary debate concerning the significance of these named individuals, see Fiorenza, 'Missionaries, Apostles, Co-workers: Romans 16 and the Reconstruction of Women's Early Christian History', in A. Loades (ed.), *Feminist Theology: A Reader*, London, SPCK, 1990, pp.57–71.

247 For detailed comments on the particular names and occupations and the social significance of them see Meeks, *Urban Christians*.

248 See above, pp.79–81.

249 See above, p.43.

250 For analysis of these factors in the development of early Christianity, see C.C. Rowland, *Christian Origins*, pp.236–308.

251 Fiorenza, *In Memory of Her*, pp.309–310.

252 The full text which includes important reference to the story of Adam and Eve will be discussed in the next section; see below, pp.149–151. This text is traditionally ascribed to Paul, but this is contested by modern biblical scholarship; see, e.g., Rowland, *Christian Origins*, pp.264–265.

253 For material on the Montanist movement and their literature, see R.E. Heine, *The Montanist Oracles and Testimonia*, Patristic Monograph

Series 14, Macon, GA, Mercer University Press, 1989; and, S. Elm, 'Montanist Oracles', in Fiorenza (ed.), *Searching the Scriptures: Vol.2*, pp.131–138.

254 For a detailed account of this text see, S. E. McGinn, 'The Acts of Thecla', in Fiorenza (ed.), *Searching the Scriptures: Vol.2*, pp.800–828.

255 See above, p.18.

256 Fiorenza, *In Memory of Her*, pp.309–315.

257 See above, p.40, and below, p.153.

258 Fiorenza, *In Memory of Her*, p.254.

259 See, e.g., *Summa Theologica*, London, Burns, Oates and Washbourne, 1922, I Q.92, art.1, Vol.IX, pp.275–276.

260 Fiorenza, *In Memory of Her*, pp.255–256.

261 See above, pp.55–56.

262 See above, pp.6–7.

263 See below, pp.132–136.

264 This verse is very significant when we find the very same theological interpretation of the Genesis creation story in a NT text: 1 Tim. 2.14; see below, pp.153–155; and Sawyer, 'Resurrecting Eve?', pp.278–279.

265 Fiorenza, *In Memory of Her*, p.253.

266 The third NT example of a household code, Eph. 5.21–69, gives the definitive theology for Christian marriage and we realize that Christianity has moved a long way away from the position in 1 Cor. 7 where Paul recommended that marriage for a Christian was not a state to be sought after. The relationship between Christ and the church is the paradigm for Christian marriage.

267 Fiorenza, *In Memory of Her*, p.262.

268 For examples, see E.A. Clark, *Women in the Early Church*, Lewiston, New York, Edwin Mellen, 1984.

269 See above, p.65.

270 This issue has been part of gender studies for the past fifty years, first clealy articulated by Simone de Beauvoir, *The Second Sex*.

271 This phenomenon is discussed above, pp.68–70, and will be given limited space in the present context.

272 *Histories*, 29.10.4–11; 8; 29.14.5–14.

273 See above, pp.53–54.

274 'The Roman and the Foreign: The Cult of the "Great Mother" in Imperial Rome', in Nicholas Thomas and Caroline Humphrey (eds), *Shamanism, History, and the State*, Michigan, University of Michigan Press, 1994, pp.168–169.

275 *Fasti* 4.179–372.

276 This legend is set in context with other accounts of ancient heroines in Fantham *et al.*, *Women in the Classical World*, pp.220–227. For the account see Suetonius, *Tiberius*, 2,3.

277 Beard, 'The Cult of the "Great Mother"', pp.169–170.

278 *ibid.*, p.172.

279 *ibid.*

280 *ibid.*, pp.172–3.

281 Prudentius, *Crowns of Martyrdom* 10.1006–1050, referred to by Beard, 'The Cult of the "Great Mother"', p.173.

282 For a detailed account of the political and social implications of the priesthoods of the Roman civic cults see R. Gordon, 'The Veil of Power: Emperors, Sacrificers and Benefactors', in Beard and North (eds), *Pagan Priests*, pp.199–231.

283 Beard, 'The Cult of the "Great Mother"', p.174.

284 *ibid.*, pp.175–176.

285 *ibid.*, p.175.

286 'Religion in the Roman Empire', in Beard and North (eds), *Pagan Priests*, p.248.

287 *ibid.*

288 Dionysius of Halicarnassus, *Roman Antiquities*, 2.19.

289 *Memorable Deeds and Sayings*, 7.6.

290 Beard, 'The Cult of the "Great Mother"', p.177.

291 *ibid.*, pp.177–178.

292 *ibid.*, p.187.

293 For example, Cato the Elder; see above, p.23.

294 Beard and North (eds), *Pagan Priests*, p.206.

295 *ibid.*, p.207.

296 See above, pp.68–70.

297 See above, p.71. The Vestal Virgins were already involved in the sense that they took part in that ritual, and had repeated the ritual in the light of the violation: Cicero, *Att.* 1, 13, 3. Here the participation of the Vestal Virgins is an example of how they not only extend the bounds of female gender expectations, but also, although being in the category of unmarried and childless women, by being part of this ritual, are regarded as 'matrons'; see Beard, 'Sexual Status of Vestal Virgins', pp.15–17.

298 Beard, 'Priesthood in the Roman Republic', in Beard and North (eds), *Pagan Priests*, p.25.

299 Mary Douglas, 'Self Evidence', in *Implicit Meanings: Essays in Anthropology*, London, Routledge, 1975.

300 See above, p.70.

301 Although in Greco-Roman religion it was not unusual to regard sexual activity as polluting for anyone participating in it, long-term celibacy was unusual; see Beard, 'Vestal Virgins', pp.12–13.

302 See above, p.69.

303 See Beard, 'Vestal Virgins', p.13.

304 See above, pp.79–81.

305 See above, p.90.

306 For an account of the wisdom tradition in Ancient Israel see Gerhard Von Rad, *Wisdom in Israel*, London, SCM Press, 1972; on *Proverbs* see William McKane's detailed commentary, *Proverbs*, London, SCM Press, 1970.

307 For exhaustive study of the use of female imagery in *Proverbs* and related literature see Claudia Camp, *Wisdom and the Feminine in the Book of Proverbs*, Sheffield, Sheffield Academic Press, 1985.

308 The Hebrew noun translated as 'wisdom' is *hokhma*, conveniently a feminine noun which allows for female personification.

309 See above, p.111.

310 These issues are discussed in A.J. Levine (ed.), '*Women Like This*', in particular, C.V. Camp's contribution, 'Understanding a Patriarchy: Women in Second Century Jerusalem Through the Eyes of Ben Sira', pp.1–39.

311 I discuss Aristotelian influence on this passage from *Sirach* in 'Resurrecting Eve?', in Morris and Sawyer (eds), *A Walk in the Garden*, pp.273–289.

312 Eve as more culpable of the two, however, is an interpretation common in Jewish as well as Christian literature, see, e.g., *Life of Adam and Eve* 7.

313 For an account of Jewish theology concerning the make-up of human nature, see E.E. Urbach, *The Sages: Their Concepts and Beliefs*, Vol.1, Jerusalem, Magnes, 1975, pp.471–483.

314 'Conflicting Images of Women in Ancient Judaism', in *Hellenism – Judaism – Christianity: Essays on their Interaction*, pp.73–95.

315 *Hypothetica* VII 3.

316 *Ant.* i 49,

317 P.W.van der Horst, *Hellenism – Judaism – Christianity*, p.95.

318 The talmudic account of this tradition is found in b.Shabb.88b-89a; see also Exodus Rabbah 33.1. It occurs as an extended excursus in *Midrash Aleph Beth* 2.11; see D.F. Sawyer, *Midrash Aleph Beth*, Atlanta, Georgia, Scholars Press, 1993, pp.105–107.

319 Judith Plaskow's presentation of feminist midrash on the Lilith tradition is a compelling illustration of this contemporary interest; see 'The Coming of Lilith', in C.P. Christ and J. Plaskow (eds), *Womanspirit Rising: A Feminist Reader in Religion*, Harper and Row, San Francisco, 1979, pp.206–207.

320 On Lilith in *Isaiah* see J.F.A. Sawyer, *The Fifth Gospel: Isaiah in the History of Christianity*, Cambridge, Cambridge University Press, 1996, pp.215–219.

321 The Lilith traditions are collected together in L. Ginzberg (ed.), *Legends of the Jews*, Vol.1, Philadelphia, Jewish Publication Society of America, 1913, pp.66ff.

322 The Babylonian Talmud describes how she can kidnap any person sleeping in a room on their own, b.Shab.151b.

323 'Lilith' in S. Sheridan (ed.), *Hear Our Voice*, p.100.

324 See above, pp.79–80.

325 See discussion of Ruth and Judith, pp.84–86 and pp.97–100.

326 'The Literary Characterization of Mother and Sexual Politics in the Hebrew Bible', in A.Y. Collins (ed.), *Feminist Perspectives on Biblical Scholarship*, Chico, California, Scholars Press, 1985, p.120.

327 Male offspring were the reproductive goal for Hebrew society, reflected, e.g., in the the purification laws regarding women after childbirth; see above, p.38.

328 E.g., the targum Ps. Jonathan on Gen. 22.20.

329 'A Mother in Israel: Aspects of the Mother Role in Jewish Myth', in R.M. Gross (ed.), *Beyond Androcentrism: New Essays on Women and Religion*, Missoula, MT, Scholars Press, 1977, pp.237–255.

330 *Gender, Power and Promise: The Subject of the Bible's First Story*, Nashville, Abingdon Press, 1993.

331 *ibid.*, p.38.

332 Adler, 'A Mother in Israel', p.244.

333 See above, pp.106–116.

334 See above, pp.109–110.

335 See above, pp.78–79.

336 See above, pp.68–70.

337 Philo, *On the Contemplative Life*, from section 68–69.

338 Gal. 3.28; see above, pp.101–103.

339 Rom. 6.3–4.

340 See, e.g., the expulsion of the Jews from Rome by Claudius in 49 CE. According to Suetonius' record this was the result of disorder among them over beliefs about 'Chrestus'; see *Life of Claudius* 25.4.

341 See above, pp.113–114.

342 A vivid description of these beliefs is given by Paul, 1 Cor. 15.23–28; also *Revelation*.

343 Rom. 5 and 1 Cor. 15.

344 I rehearsed these arguments for the first time in an earlier article, Morris and Sawyer (eds), *A Walk in the Garden*, pp. 271–289.

345 The question regarding women's hair-style in Corinth is discussed above, pp.103–105.

346 *Discourse 2 on Genesis*, translation from Elizabeth A. Clark, *Women in the Early Church*, pp.35–36. All translations from the Church Fathers in this section are taken from Clark.

347 This observation applies to certain other Pauline texts where there are passages that are central to the debate concerning the status of women, namely, Colossians, Ephesians and the other pastoral epistles: 2 Timothy and Titus.

348 Fiorenza, *In Memory of Her*, pp.251–284; see above, pp.111–115.

349 See above, pp.110–113.

350 On Augustine's ideas concerning sexual hierarchy see Genevieve Lloyd, 'Augustine and Aquinas', in Ann Loades (ed.), *Feminist Theology: A Reader*, pp.90–8.

351 *Literal Commentary on Genesis*, IX,5.

352 Translation from H. Rackham, *Aristotle, Politics*, Loeb Classical Library, Cambridge, Mass., Harvard University Press, 1926; see the discussion of household codes above, pp.110–113.

353 *The Kind of Women Who Ought to be Taken as Wives* 4.

354 The same tendency is evidenced in the Jewish apocryphal work *Sirach*; see above, pp.134–135.

355 For a critique of Christianity's understanding of woman as the 'other', with its focus on Eve, see Mary Daly, *Beyond God the Father: Toward a Philosophy of Women's Liberation*, Boston, Beacon Press, 1974, pp.13–68.

356 Ambrose, *On Paradise*, XII, 56.

357 Augustine, *Literal Commentary on Genesis*, XI,42.

358 *Against Heresies*, III,22,4.

359 This same theology is heard in the following poem:

> Ne had the apple taken been
> The apple taken been,
> Ne hadde never our Lady
> A been heaven's queen.
> Blessed be the time
> That apple taken was!
> Therefore we may singen
> 'Deo Gratias!'

From the work of a fifteenth-century anonymous poet; Helen Gardner (ed.), *Oxford Book of English Verse 1250–1950*, Oxford, Oxford University Press, 1972, pp.13–14.

360 See above, pp.5–7.
361 In relation to current feminist dialogue with classical philosophy and gender theory see J. Butler, *Bodies that Matter: On the Discursive Limits of Sex*, London, Routledge, 1993, pp.27–55.
362 For examples of contemporary feminist spirituality see U. King, *Women and Spirituality: Voices of Protest and Promise*, London, Macmillan, 1993; K. Zappone, *The Hope for Wholeness: A Spirituality for Feminists*, Mystic, Connecticut, Twenty-Third Publications, 1991; J. Plaskow and C.P. Christ (eds), *Weaving the Visions: New Patterns in Feminist Spirituality*, New York, HarperSan Francisco, 1989.

BIBLIOGRAPHY

Adler, R., 'A Mother in Israel: Aspects of the Mother Role in Jewish Myth', in R.M. Gross (ed.), *Beyond Androcentrism, New Essays on Women and Religion*, Missoula, MT, Scholar Press, 1977.
—— 'The Virgin in the Brothel and Other Anomalies: Character and Context in the Legend of Beruria', *Tikkun*, 3.6 (1989).
Archer, L.J., 'Bound by Blood: Circumcision and Menstrual Taboo in Post Exilic Judaism', in J. Martin-Soskice (ed.), *After Eve: Women, Theology and Judaeo-Christian Tradition*, London, Marshall Pickering, 1989.
—— *Her Price Beyond Rubies*, Sheffield, Sheffield Academic Press, 1990.
Arthur, M.B., 'Politics and Pomegranates: An Interpretation of the Homeric Hymn to Demeter', *Arethusa*, 10 (1977), 7–47.
Balsdon, J.P.V.D., *Roman Women: Their History and Habits*, London, The Bodley Head, 1962.
—— *Life and Leisure in Ancient Rome*, London, The Bodley Head, 1969.
Baskin, J. (ed.), *Jewish Women in Historical Perspective*, Detroit, Wayne State University Press, 1991.
Bauman, R.A., *Women and Politics in Ancient Rome*, London, Rout-ledge,1992.
Beard, M., 'The Sexual Status of Vestal Virgins', *Journal of Roman Studies*, 70 (1980), 12–27.
—— and North, J. (eds), *Pagan Priests: Religion and Power in the Ancient World*, London, Duckworth, 1990.
—— 'The Roman and the Foreign: The Cult of the "Great Mother" in Imperial Rome', in Nicholas Thomas and Caroline Humphrey (eds), *Shamanism, History, and the State*, Michigan, University of Michigan Press, 1994, pp.168–169.
Beauvoir, S. de, *The Second Sex*, London, Picador, 1949/1988.
Boulding, E., *The Underside of History: A View of Women Through Time*, Boulder, Colorado, Westview Press, 1976.
Brenner, A., *A Feminist Companion to Ruth*, Sheffield, Sheffield Academic Press, 1993.
Brooten, B.J., *Women Leaders in the Ancient Synagogue: Inscriptional Evidence and Background Issues*, Brown Judaic Studies No. 36, Atlanta, Georgia, Scholars Press, 1982.

Brouwer, H.H.J., *Bona Dea: The Sources and a Description of the Cult*, EPRO 110, Leiden, Brill, 1989.

Brown, P., *The Body and Society: Men, Women and Sexual Renunciation in Early Christianity*, London, Faber and Faber, 1988.

Brown, R.E., Fitzmyer, J.A. and Murphy, R.E., *The New Jerome Biblical Commentary*, London, Geoffrey Chapman, 1991.

Butler, J., *Bodies that Matter: On the Discursive Limits of Sex*, London, Routledge, 1993.

Camp, C., *Wisdom and the Feminine in the Book of Proverbs*, Sheffield, Sheffield Academic Press, 1985.

Christ, C.P. and Plaskow, J. (eds), *Womanspirit Rising: A Feminist Reader in Religion*, San Francisco, Harper and Row, 1979.

Clark, E.A., *Women in the Early Church*, Lewiston, NY, Edwin Mellen, 1984.

Cole Guettel, S., 'New Evidence for the Mysteries of Dionysius', *GRBS*, 21 (1980) 3, 223–238.

Collins, A.Y. (ed.), *Feminist Perspectives on Biblical Scholarship*, Chico, California, Scholars Press, 1985.

Daly, M., *Beyond God the Father: Toward a Philosophy of Women's Liberation*, Boston, Beacon Press, 1973.

Dill, S., *Roman Society: From Nero to Marius Aurelius*, Cleveland and New York, Meridian, 1956.

Dixon, S., *The Roman Mother*, London, Routledge, 1990.

Douglas, M., 'Self Evidence', in *Implicit Meanings: Essays in Anthropology*, London, Routledge, 1975.

Dowden, K., *Religion and the Romans*, London, Bristol Classical Press, 1992.

Doyle, J.A. and Paludi, M.A., *Sex and Gender: The Human Experience*, Dubuque, Iowa, William C. Brown Publishers, 2nd ed., 1991.

Evans, J.K., *War, Women and Children in Ancient Rome*, London, Routledge, 1991.

Fantham, E., Foley, H.P., Kampen, N.B., Pomeroy, S.B. and Shapiro, H.A. (eds), *Women in the Classical World*, Oxford, Oxford University Press, 1994.

Fewell, D. and Gunn, D., *Gender, Power and Promise: The Subject of the Bible's First Story*, Nashville, Abingdon Press, 1993.

Fiorenza, E. Schüssler, *In Memory of Her: A Feminist Theological Reconstruction of Christian Origins*, London, SCM Press, 1983.

—— (ed.), *Searching the Scriptures Volume 2: A Feminist Commentary*, London, SCM Press, 1995.

Fuller, E. (ed.), *Plutarch: Lives of the Noble Romans*, London, Penguin, 1959.

Gardner, H. (ed.), *Oxford Book of English Verse 1250–1950*, Oxford, Oxford University Press, 1972.

Ginzberg, L. (ed.), *Legends of the Jews*, Vol.1, Philadelphia, Jewish Publication Society of America, 1913.

Goldfeld, A., *Women as Sources of Torah in the Rabbinic Tradition*, New York, Shocken Books, 1976.

Graham, E., *Making the Difference: Gender, Personhood and Theology*, London, Mowbray, 1995.

Graves, R. (ed.), *The Transformations of Lucius otherwise known as the Golden Ass, by Apuleius*, New York, Farrer Straus, 1951.

Green, W. (ed.), *Persons and Institutions in Early Rabbinic Judaism*, Missoula, MT, Scholars Press, 1977.

Greenburg, B., 'Female Sexuality and Bodily Functions in the Jewish Tradition', in J. Becher (ed.), *Women, Religion and Sexuality*, Geneva, WCC Publications, 1990.

Grossman, S. and Haut, R., *Daughters of the King: Women and the Synagogue*, Philadelphia, New York, Jerusalem, The Jewish Publication Society, 1992.

Hallet, J.P., *Fathers and Daughters in Roman Society*, Princeton, Princeton University Press, 1984.

Hampson, D., *Theology and Feminism*, Oxford, Blackwell, 1990.

Heine, R.E., *The Montanist Oracles and Testimonia*, Patrisitic Monograph Series 14, Macon, GA, Mercer University Press, 1989.

Heyob, S.K., *The Cult of Isis among Women in the Greco-Roman World*, Leiden, Brill, 1975.

Horst, P.W. van der, *Hellenism – Judaism – Christianity: Essays on their Interaction*, Kampen, The Netherlands, Kok Pharos, 1994.

Kampen, N., *Image and Status: Roman Working Women in Ostia*, Berlin, Mann, 1981.

King, U., *Women and Spirituality: Voices of Protest and Promise*, London, Macmillan, 1993.

Kraemer, R. S. (ed.), *Maenads, Martyrs, Matrons, Monastics: A Sourcebook on Women's Religion in the Greco-Roman World*, Philadelphia, Fortress Press, 1988.

—— *Her Share of the Blessings: Women's Religions Among Pagans, Jews, and Christians in the Greco-Roman World*, Oxford, Oxford University Press, 1992.

LaCocque, A., *The Feminine Unconventional: Four Subversive Figures in Israel's Tradition*, Minneapolis, Fortress Press, 1990.

Lefkowitz, M.R. and Fant, M.B., *Women's Lives in Greece and Rome: A Source Book in Translation*, Baltimore, Johns Hopkins University Press, 1982.

Levine, A.J. (ed.), *'Women Like This': New Perspectives on Jewish Women in the Greco-Roman World*, Atlanta, Scholars Press, 1991.

Lewis, C.T. and Short, C., *A Latin Dictionary*, Oxford, Oxford University Press, 1879.

Liebeschuetz, J.H.W.G., *Continuity and Change in Roman Religion*, Oxford, Oxford University Press, 1979.

Lincoln, B., *Emerging from the Chrysalis: Studies in Rituals of Women's Initiation*, Cambridge, Mass., Harvard University Press, 1981.

Loades, A. (ed.), *Feminist Theology: A Reader*, London, SPCK, 1990.

Lorde, A., 'The Master's Tools Will Never Dismantle the Master's House', in C. Moraga and G. Anzaldua (eds), *This Bridge Called My Back: Writings by Radical Women of Color*, Watertown, MA, Persephone Press, 1981.

McKane, W., *Proverbs*, London, SCM Press, 1970.

Magie, D., trans., *Scriptores Historiae Augustae: Thirty Pretenders*, Loeb Classical Library, Cambridge, Mass., Harvard University Press, 1967–1968.

Magonet, J., 'A Note on Leviticus 12.5', in J.F.A. Sawyer (ed.), *Reading Leviticus: Responses to Mary Douglas and Other Inter-Disciplinary Approaches*, Sheffield, Sheffield Academic Press, 1996.

Marchant, E.C. and Bowersock, G.W., trans., *Xenophon VII. Scripta Minora*, Loeb Classical Library, Cambridge, Mass., Harvard University Press, 1968.

Meeks, W., *The First Urban Christians: The Social World of the Apostle Paul*, New Haven, Yale University Press, 1983.

—— *The Moral World of the First Christians*, London, SPCK, 1987.

Morris, P. and Sawyer, D.F. (eds), *A Walk in the Garden: Biblical, Iconographical and Literary Images of Eden*, Sheffield, Sheffield Academic Press, 1992.

Neusner, J., *The Idea of Purity in Ancient Judaism, with critique and commentary by M. Douglas*, Leiden, Brill, 1973.

—— *Judaism and Christianity in the Age of Constantine: History, Messiah, Israel, and the Initial Confrontation*, Chicago, University of Chicago Press, 1987.

—— *Introduction to Rabbinic Literature*, New York, Doubleday, 1994.

Nickelsburg, G., *Jewish Literature Between the Bible and the Mishnah: A Historical and Literary Introduction*, Philadelphia, Fortress Press, 1981.

Plaskow, J., 'The Coming of Lilith', in C.P. Christ and J. Plaskow (eds), *Womanspirit Rising: A Feminist Reader in Religion*, San Francisco, Harper and Row, 1979, pp.206–207.

Plaskow, J. and Christ, C.P. (eds), *Weaving the Visions: New Patterns in Feminist Spirituality*, New York, HarperSan Francisco, 1989.

Pomeroy, S., *Goddesses, Whores, Wives and Slaves: Women in Classical Antiquity*, New York, Shocken Books, 1975.

Rackham, H., trans., *Politics*, Loeb Classical Library, Cambridge, Mass., Harvard University Press, 1926.

Rawson, B., *The Family in Ancient Rome: New Perspectives*, London, Routledge, 1992.

Rhode, D.L. (ed.), *Theoretical Perspectives on Sexual Difference*, New Haven, Yale University Press, 1990.

Rowland, C.C., *Christian Origins: An Account of the Setting and Character of the Most Important Messianic Sect of Judaism*, London, SPCK, 1985.

Ruether, R.R., *Sexism and God-Talk: Towards a Feminist Theology*, London, SCM Press, 1983.

—— *Gaia and God: An Ecofeminist Theology of Earth Healing*, London, SCM Press, 1992.

Russell, L. (ed.), *Feminist Interpretation of the Bible*, Oxford, Blackwell, 1985.

Sanders, E.P., *Judaism: Practice and Belief 63 BCE– 66 CE*, London, SCM Press, 1992.

Sanders, J.T., *Schismatics, Sectarians, Dissidents, Deviants: The First One Hundred Years of Jewish–Christian Relations*, London, SCM Press, 1993.

Saunders, T.J., 'Plato on Women in the Laws', in A. Powell (ed.), *The Greek World*, 2nd ed., London, Routledge, 1995, pp.591–609.

Sawyer, D.F., 'The Story of Mary: Luke's Version', *New Blackfriars*, December 1989, pp.555–564.

—— 'Resurrecting Eve', in P. Morris and D.F. Sawyer (eds), *A Walk in the Garden*, Sheffield, Sheffield Academic Press, 1992.

—— *Midrash Aleph Beth*, Atlanta, Georgia, Scholars Press, 1993.

Sawyer, J.F.A., *The Fifth Gospel: Isaiah in the History of Christianity*, Cambridge, Cambridge University Press, 1996.

Schor, N. and Weed, E. (eds) *The Essential Difference*, Bloomington and Indianapolis, Indiana University Press, 1994.

Schulz, F., *Classical Roman Law*, Oxford, Oxford University Press, 1951.

Schürer, E., *The History of the Jewish People in the Age of Jesus Christ*, 4 vols, revised and edited by G. Vermes, F. Millar, M. Goodman and M. Black, Edinburgh, T & T Clark, 1973–1986.

Scullard, H.H., *A History of the Roman World 753 to 146* BC, London, Routledge, 1980.

Segal, P., 'The Penalty of the Warning Inscription from the Temple of Jerusalem', Jerusalem, *Israel Exploration Journal*, 39 (1989), 79–84.

Sheridan, S. (ed.), *Hear Our Voice: Women Rabbis Tell their Stories*, London, SCM Press, 1994.

Snyder, J., *The Woman and the Lyre: Women Writers in Classical Greece and Rome*, Carbondale, Southern Illinois University Press, 1989.

Stone, M., *Scriptures, Sects and Visions: A Profile of Judaism from Ezra to the Jewish Revolts*, Philadelphia, Fortress Press, 1980.

Strack, H.L., *Introduction to the Talmud and Midrash*, New York, Atheneum, 1969.

Swidler, L.J., *Women in Judaism: The Status of Women in Formative Judaism*, New Jersey, Scarecrow Press, Metuchen, 1976.

Talbert, R., *Plutarch on Sparta*, London, Penguin, 1988.

Theissen, G., *Sociology of Early Palestinian Christianity*, Philadelphia, Fortress Press, 1978.

Thomas, N. and Humphrey, C. (eds), *Shamanism, History, and the State*, Michigan, University of Michigan Press, 1994.

Trebilco, P.R., *Jewish Communities in Asia Minor*, Cambridge, Cambridge University Press, 1991.

Trible, P., *God and the Rhetoric of Sexuality*, Philadelphia, Fortress Press, 1979.

Ulansey, D., *The Origins of the Mithraic Mysteries: Cosmology and Salvation in the Ancient World*, Oxford, Oxford University Press, 1989.

Urbach, E.E., *The Sages: Their Concepts and Beliefs*, Vol.1, Jerusalem, Magnes, 1975.

Von Rad, G., *Wisdom in Israel*, London, SCM Press, 1972.

Wegner, J.R., *Chattel or Person? The Status of Women in the Mishnah*, Oxford, Oxford University Press, 1988.

Witherington, B., *Women and the Genesis of Christianity*, Cambridge, Cambridge University Press, 1990.

Wright, N.T., *The New Testament and the People of God*, Vol.1, London, SPCK, 1993.

Zappone, K., *The Hope for Wholeness: A Spirituality for Feminists*, Mystic, Connecticut, Twenty-Third Publications, 1991.

INDEX

Camp, C. 172 (note 307), 173 (note 310)
Canaan 49
Caria 79f.
castration 70, 105, 120–2, 124
Cato the Elder 14, 23f., 64f., 162 (note 61), 166 (note 150), 172 (note 293)
celibacy 21, 69, 106, 109
Cenchreae 67
Christ 101, 103, 106, 108, 111, 116, 148f., 153–7
Christ, C.P. 175 (note 362)
Chrysostom, John 1 (note 2), 150f., 153
Cicero 34, 71, 172 (note 297)
circumcision 35f., 141
Clark, E.A. 160 (note 2), 171 (note 268), 174 (note 346)
Clement of Rome 97
Clodius 71
Cole, S. Guettel 166 (note 146)
Colossians, Letter to 110, 115, 148f., 174 (note 347)
Columella 28
Constantine 41
Corinth 29f.
Corinthians, Letters to 101–7, 110, 115, 150f., 153, 168 (note 203), 169 (note 204), 170 (note 245), 171 (note 266), 174 (note 342)
Cornelia 21, 25
Court of Women 73f., 77f.
Crete 79f.
Cumae 53
Cybele, see Magna Mater

Daly, M. 161 (note 13), 174 (note 355)
Dead Sea Scrolls 83
Deborah 98f.
Demeter 4, 57, 59–61, 85, 158f.
Deuteronomy 164 (notes 91–6)
Diana 53
Dio Chrysostomus 163 (note 67)
Diodorus 166 (note 144)
Dionysius of Halicarnassus 172 (note 288)
Dionysus 47, 61–4

Dixon, S. 22
Douglas, M. 127, 164 (note 88), 172 (note 299)
Dowden, K. 50
Doyle, J.A. 160 (note 5)

education 21f., 27
El 49
Elder, L.B. 170 (note 235)
Eleusis 59f.
emancipation 19–21, 26, 31, 55
Ephesians, Letter to 10, 110, 151, 171 (note 266), 174 (note 347)
Esau 142f.
eschatology 106–8
Essenes 79, 83
eunuchs 121, 123
Euripides 62–4
Evans, J.K. 161 (note 26)
Eve 116, 134f., 142f., 145, 149–57, 159
Exodus, Book of 82

Fant, M.B. 161 (note 18)
Fantham, E. 161 (note 119), 165 (notes 121, 125, 127)
Fauna 71
Faunus 71
feminism 7, 55, 60, 85f., 127, 138f., 141
Fewell, D. 142f.
Fiorenza, E. Schussler 45, 93, 97, 100, 104f., 107, 110–13, 151, 165 (note 115), 169 (notes 215, 221, 223, 226), 170 (notes 235, 240f., 243, 246, 251, 253), 171 (notes 254, 256, 258, 260, 265, 267), 174 (note 348)
Fuchs, E. 141

Galatians, Letter to 101, 147, 170 (note 240), 174 (note 338)
galli 105, 121–4, 129
Gardner, H. 175 (note 359)
gender theory 3–8, 47f., 66, 117–18, 126–9, 144f., 157, 175 (note 361)
Genesis, Book of 134, 141–3, 150–6, 164 (note 84)
Genucius 123